ENGLAND'S
LAST GLORY

THE BOYS OF '66

David Miller

Foreword by
Franz Beckenbauer

PAVILION

First published in the United Kingdom in 1986 by Pavilion Books
151 Freston Road
London
W10 6TH

An Imprint of Anova Books Company Ltd

This updated paperback edition first published in United Kingdom
in 2006.

Picture research by Mick Alexander
Designed by Lawrence Edwards
Cover designed by Lotte Oldfield

ISBN 1 86205 729 X

A CIP catalogue record for this book is available
from the British Library

2 4 6 8 10 9 7 5 3

Typeset by SX Composing DTP Ltd, England
Printed by MPG Books Ltd, England

www.anovabooks.com

OTHER DAVID MILLER TITLES PUBLISHED BY PAVILION

Father of Football
A biography of Matt Busby
Olympic Revolution
A biography of Juan Antonio Samaranch
Our Sporting Times
Born to Run
A Biography of Sebastian Coe

Contents

For Max

Foreword by Franz Beckenbauer

President of Bayern Munich FC, the only man to captain and manage winning World Cup teams (1974 and 1990), Chairman of FIFA World Cup Organising Committee 2006

The World Cup Final of 1966 remains, in Germany, one of the great talking points, even today, forty years later. Was it, or wasn't it, the third goal for England? People still argue. I think that's a shame, because it reduces some of England's glory. To be truthful, England were the better team, over 90 minutes and then in extra time. There's no argument. They deserved the trophy.

We had been lucky with our second goal, to draw level 2-2 moments from the end of normal time: first, with the free-kick given against Jack Charlton, and then the deflections and a scrambled goal-mouth shot. At the time of England's third goal, I was in the penalty area, with quite a good view. I was convinced the ball touched the goal-line – was not completely over – when Geoff Hurst's shot bounced down from the cross-bar, and that it was therefore not a goal. What language did the Swiss referee and the Russian linesman use when they discussed the incident? Who said what? We'll never know.

It was my first World Cup. I remember that it was well organised, and there were big crowds almost everywhere. It was such a huge opportunity for a youngster like me, to play in front of the whole world, with the recent advances in television. You need such an event, a World Cup or a European Championship, to help build your career. That tournament enabled me to become well-known, a star as they say, so I was grateful that we should have such a memorable final against the host nation.

Before the match, Helmut Schoen, our manager, and his assistant coaches, decided that I should mark Bobby Charlton. They knew that if I did, it would reduce my own strength for attacking, but they were insistent. 'It's very important', Schoen said, 'because you're fast enough to stay with him, to control him'. Bobby at that time was the best player in the world, and he also had lungs like a horse. I never remember being so exhausted as I was at the finish that afternoon.

Playing the role I did on that day meant that neither of us could really enjoy the match, neutralising each other. At that time, I played in midfield for the national team, and did so until 1971, but with my club, Bayern, I had played as *libero*, or sweeper as you call it, since 1964. I preferred that. It was an easier way to play, with more freedom. I didn't like man-for-man, pinned down the whole time in a specialised function, which was then the system throughout Europe. I preferred *libero,* where I felt I could have more influence on a game, instead of a duel against a single opponent. I know how much Netzer and Overath, playing in midfield, used to complain about this aspect of the game.

Whereas England had a slice of luck in 1966, I think we did in the quarter-final in 1970. After an hour, with England leading 2-0, we were completely dead. We had not had a single chance. It was unfortunate that England had lost Gordon Banks in goal, through illness. After I had scored what I thought was rather a soft goal, to make it 2-1, Alf Ramsey decided to substitute Bobby Charlton, who we felt was the heart of the game. We started to play better and eventually Gerd Müller won us the match. Yet I thought that this England team was even stronger than in 1966, especially with attacking full-backs in Cooper and Newton. If England had beaten us then, they would have been in the final against Brazil. And then, who knows?

It is good to read again about the excitement of 1966, and all the names that were involved. David Miller, who over many years has been a regular and welcome visitor to Germany's training camps and matches, is well qualified to tell the story.

Franz Beckenbauer

Introduction

THE MOST CELEBRATED day in the history of British sport, the winning of the World Cup at Wembley by Alf Ramsey's team on 30th July, 1966, is now more than half a life-time away. For those old enough to have first-hand recollection, many of the facts, even the extent of the emotion experienced throughout the country, may have become faded and blurred. For anyone born, say, in 1956 or after – and therefore ten or less at the time of the match – it is not much more than some historical event alongside other milestones in the history books, such as 1066. For those of us who ached with anxiety at the time, with the thrill of ultimate achievement, who were moved by the mastery of Bobby Moore, the exhilarating sight of Bobby Charlton in full flow, or the unique spectacle of the recently-arrived Geoff Hurst scoring a winning hat-trick against West Germany, there can never be another moment like it. English reserve dissolved, and the celebrations had London throbbing all night to the sound of incessant car horns. For a few hours, we behaved almost like Brazilians. It is the memory of the *pleasure* given to us by eleven footballers, who were so definitively a team, that will never perish for those of us fortunate enough to have been there or to have witnessed it live on television.

For all nations it is a spontaneous, natural emotion to yearn for success in sport. It is collectively reassuring; it gives pride and pleasure in a subjective way, especially with team events, in which we particularly feel that the team is representing us. It is a more personal thing for the spectators than with an individual's achievement. At such moments, the team become brothers to us all, so that the affection in which Moore and his colleagues were held continued long after the impact of their triumph had disappeared.

This was to be so abundantly evident with the sad and premature death of Bobby Moore in February 1993, at the age of only fifty-one. With a combination of privacy and dignity that had characterised his behaviour in all spheres from an early age, he had withheld for several years, from all but a few close friends, the fact that he had cancer of the stomach. When this fatally spread to his liver, and being conscious that the decline in his health would become visible, he discreetly revealed his plight in order to deflect anxious inquiries and to deaden the extent of speculative gossip. With that undemonstrative fortitude that we had seen throughout his playing career, he continued to attempt to lead a normal life, and indeed a short time before he died was back at the scene of his greatest hour to watch England play at Wembley against San Marino. He probably knew there would not be another time. Yet among friends and acquaintances who were also there, he showed none of the inner turmoil that he must have been suffering. As on the pitch in moments of crisis, there was no flicker of anxiety. His temperament was as steady as ever.

His passing touched the heart of the nation, not just because he was too young to die but because, probably, many people suddenly realised that they had not appreciated him sufficiently while he was alive, that his greatness as a performer had been taken for granted. Because he was quiet, controlled and private, he seldom made the news when off the field. This he managed to achieve in spite of being a convivial man. Bobby was always one of those who was last out of the bar, often in the small hours – nothing extravagant, usually a quiet string of lagers – but then first in for training in the morning. He was the strong silent type, who led by example more than eloquence. There have been few sportsmen of his stature who, without ever being precious or self-conscious, managed to retain such a quietly responsible bearing in all circumstances. Never was this more apparent than when he was held under house arrest in Bogota for five days, falsely accused of stealing a bracelet from a boutique in the foyer of the team's hotel, during England's friendly match against Colombia immediately preceding the defence of their title in Mexico in 1970. Of six sets of fingerprints on the jeweller's glass cabinet from where the bracelet was allegedly removed, none were Moore's: a fact which the Bogota police had known from the outset before finally releasing him. Moore hastened to re-join the team in Mexico, and from his demeanour you would never have supposed he had been delayed by anything worse than collecting his luggage. He proceeded to play with an authority that drew even more admiration than four years previously. After an unforgettable encounter with Brazil in the first round, which England unluckily lost by the only goal, Pelé would say: 'Bobby

Moore has proved himself to be one of the most important figures who ever played the game.' So complete was the tactical control of Ramsey's team, superior in my opinion to 1966, that Brazil's respect, indeed fear, of Moore and his colleagues was as genuine as England's of Brazil.

When friends and admirers filled Westminster Abbey for Moore's memorial service, they were paying tribute to a performer's heroic style that was unique of its kind. Such had been his judgement on the field of every swirling crisis, that he possessed a serenity which left others in awe. That inimitable manager of Celtic, Jock Stein, had once said: 'There should be a law against him. He knows what's happening 20 minutes before anybody else.' Scotland had encountered this phenomenon too often for comfort. That serenity in action was equalled by his humility off the field. It was recognition of these qualities that generated a national sense of loss when illness became the only crisis to which he had no answer.

It was shamefully negligent that the Football Association had never recognised, once Moore had retired from the game, what exceptional service he might have given, to them and to the game as a whole, in some ambassadorial appointment: indeed, but for his death, as chairman of an organisation so woefully short of leadership. There has been talk of Franz Beckenbauer, Moore's illustrious contemporary and rival with Germany, and currently chairman of Bayern Munich, becoming president of FIFA. What dereliction of opportunity it was to fail to use Bobby Moore's exemplary qualities in his later years. It was not unduly sentimental when Jeff Powell of the *Daily Mail*, a close friend of Moore's, wrote in his obituary: 'God can tell Heaven's Eleven to start getting changed. The captain has arrived.'

Over the subsequent years since the illustrious era led by Moore and Bobby Charlton, England have occasionally played well but never with the same degree of authority. A succession of team managers have tried and failed to recapture the co-ordination, the fundamental team ethic, which Ramsey created. Ramsey, who had previously made wine out of water when guiding unfashionable Ipswich to promotion and then League title, understood better than any that a national team, even more than a club team – because it plays so comparatively infrequently – is dependent on the qualities of character as much as technique. This account of England's triumph tries to show, among other aspects of the competition in 1966, how exceptional was the integration and unity that Ramsey built. Of course, a national team's success is partially dependent on the individual skill of the players available. Subsequent managers have not had, as did Ramsey, five world-class players of the calibre of Gordon Banks,

Moore, Ray Wilson, Greaves and Bobby Charlton. By 1970, Alan Ball, Martin Peters and Geoff Hurst were of the same calibre. Yet equally fundamental is that quality of dependability, of being sure what a player will give you in the most pressurised circumstances on a minimum of collective training. Most of the subsequent managers – Don Revie, Ron Greenwood, Bobby Robson, Graham Taylor, Glen Hoddle, Kevin Keegan, Sven Goran Eriksson – have tended to snatch at straws, too frequent in their team changes to the detriment of continuity. Certainly, they have been short of great players, but this fact has been magnified by fluctuations in both system and personnel. Although enduring similar hostility from press and public as Ramsey did during the preparations for 1966, Terry Venables, the appointed manager in 1994, attempted to emulate Ramsey's emphasis on dependability.

What national managers and coaches tend to overlook, certainly those in charge of England, is that the functions of club and national manager are exact opposites. On the one hand, the club coach, having a limited number of say twenty players, must devise a formation or tactical system that best exploits the abilities of those players. On the other, the national manager, though having call upon perhaps fifty or sixty players, must first decide upon what he regards as the best formation for international tournaments, and then select the players to fit that system, even though they may not be the most talented players as perceived by the public. Maintaining a predetermined formation and system is the only means by which the national manager can achieve continuity, because he has access to the players so infrequently. Constantly to change the personnel and indeed the system, as many England coaches have done, is merely to increase the uncertainty, the players being unfamiliar to deliver what is required of them. When it can take a new player half a season to adjust to a club team, it is no surprise that national players are erratic in an international tournament when their colleagues are constantly altering.

Venables, who had established his coaching reputation primarily with Barcelona, having himself played for Chelsea, Spurs and England, was appointed in 1994 on the unanimous recommendation to the FA from a body of other England managers. And when confronted, for example, by the repeated cry from the media for the inclusion of Matthew Le Tissier of Southampton, a spectacular but unpredictable striker, who it was claimed 'is a match winner on his day', Venables' response was curt. 'I cannot afford to wait to find out whether it will be his day' he said. Look at Venables' team sheets and they were consistent: Seaman in goal; Garry Neville and Pearce at full back, with Adams and Southgate in central defence; Ince and Gascoigne in central mid-field between McManaman and Anderson on the flanks; Shearer and Sheringham as strikers. The team played to a predictable pattern, and with any change in individuals, those introduced were familiar with the formation. Pilloried for a goalless draw with Norway in Oslo in the autumn of 1995, Venables held his course. Between then and a semi-final with Germany in Euro '96, England won six and drew six of twelve matches, with a goal aggregate of 19 to 5, including seven defensive blank sheets, finally losing to Germany only on penalties.

Yet having requested the FA in January for an extension of his contract from 1996 to embrace the World Cup in 1998, he was shabbily rebuffed, the FA influenced by Noel White from Liverpool, member of the wholly non-functional "International Selection Committee". As Venables observed, they only wanted to bet on him after his 1996 horse had crossed the finishing line. The FA, for their part, had been concerned about widespread criticism of Venables' business affairs while manager of Tottenham from 1987 to 1991 – even though he would hold zero financial responsibility as England coach. Given their advance refusal, Venables said he would not continue, irrespective of the summer's outcome – notwithstanding that, in the event, England defeated Scotland, following an initial draw with Switzerland, then hammered Holland 4-1, were next a shade lucky to defeat Spain 4-2 on penalties in the quarter final after a goalless 120 minutes, and were equivalent to Germany, eventual winners, in the semi final.

'The victory in '66 showed you it *had* to be a team game,' Venables, who was a member of the initial squad of 40 preparing under Ramsey, said. 'The players had to be prepared and willing to put the team first. There was a tremendous spirit in the group. Alf had said, provocatively, that England would win, and they did. The players believed in him. It was a big disappointment for me that I didn't get into the final twenty-two. There were a number of players who were in the queue in front of me, and I thought Alf was right in those he selected. I'd played a couple of times, then got injured, and Johnny Byrne got back in. I don't think the timing of   my move from Chelsea to Spurs prior to the Cup helped my chances'. Venables, who from the earliest stage of his career was intent on listening, discussing and learning, would undoubtedly have profited from an association with a coach as far-sighted and simultaneously pragmatic as Ramsey.

'I can see now where I was sitting the afternoon that we won,' Venables recalls. 'I thought we *played* so well, besides winning the match. I know there was controversy over the fact that Alf played without wingers in the later stages. But the fact is that if you play with two central strikers [Hurst and Hunt], then if you also have two wingers, you'll get overrun, at the top level of international football.' Venables is convinced that the system of split strikers, one playing in behind the other – not dissimilar from the partnership of Hurst, the target man, and Hunt – is the most effective way of playing. He cites the fact that 17 of the 24 finalists in the 1994 World Cup operated this system, Brazil being the most successful. Venables is also convinced that, besides using split central strikers, the success of the best teams is built on the use of triangles. Going back to the Scots at the start of the century, that philosophy is, of course, almost as old as the game itself, epitomised by the Hungarians in the '50s, currently by Arsenal under Arsene Wenger and by Brazil whenever they have won the World Cup. The change nowadays from Ramsey's time, Venables emphasises, is that more than ever the game has to be controlled from the back, hence the necessity for greater strength in midfield.

Venables played in Tottenham's FA Cup-winning side of 1967, part of that period when Spurs were in their prime under the direction of Bill Nicholson, himself an outstanding wing-half when Spurs won the Championship in the push-and-run era – triangles! – of Arthur Rowe in the early '50s. Nicholson was denied more than his one international cap by the concurrent pre-eminence of Billy Wright. The bottom line for Nicholson was that ultimately the performance of any team lies in the skill of the players available. 'I don't think football is tied down to any set system,' Nicholson said. 'Everything so much depends on the players. If they play well, consistently, you'll win something. Alf was a bit unlucky, not winning again in 1970, just the way we were at Tottenham, not doing the Double for the second year running in 1962. The problem, always, is that you lose some matches you should win, and vice versa. Occasionally, a club or a country has exceptional players, and that way they win more often. Winning is more the result of having good players than good systems, though of course you can have the best players and not win, like Holland in the World Cup of 1974.'

Glenn Hoddle, selected to succeed Venables, had been a talented if enigmatic player for England: a refined mid-field technician, but liable to fade on tense occasions; leaving Ron Greenwood, for example, unconvinced about his inclusion during 1980-82, though Hoddle would be a regular for two seasons subsequently under Bobby Robson. Hoddle later established a coaching reputation, though his England appointment was, to say the least, speculative, given his lack of international coaching experience. With the difficult hurdle of Italy in a World Cup qualifying group, he lost the first leg at home 1-0 – with a team showing five changes from the previous tie in Georgia – but against expectation gained a crucial goalless draw in Rome.

In the finals in France, England lost erratically to Romania, squeezing into the second round with victories over Tunisia and Colombia, only then to lose on penalties to Argentina at the end of a 2-2 draw, the rapidly emerging David Beckham having been disruptively sent off for a relatively insignificant flip of the foot when lying face down on the turf. The next season, Hoddle dug his own grave with some imprudent religion-orientated comments, disparaging to the disabled – pruriently exploited by *The Times* when Hoddle's views had been previously publicised – on account of which the FA felt compelled to terminate his reign.

The inter-regnum appointment was Kevin Keegan, an assignation even more speculative, given Keegan's known emotional instability, as witnessed when in charge of Newcastle. Keegan, who rose to eminence as a player with Liverpool and Hamburg and had vigorously captained England, had built a notable career by determined application of less than exceptional skills. No one surpassed his enthusiasm, but his handling of England was always tremulous. Though defeating an equally uncertain Germany in the second of three first-round matches in the finals of Euro 2000, England stumbled against both Portugal and Romania for an undignified exit. Only two matches on, in the autumn, and they lost 1-0 at home to Germany in a World Cup qualifier, whereupon Keegan histrionically resigned that night, never mind that England faced a further tie four days later in Finland – for which Howard Wilkinson was made emergency coach.

Losing two managers within two years was an embarrassment for the FA. Adam Crozier, their recently appointed new chief executive, possibly seeking to be dramatic yet having no depth of football experience, convinced his employers it was worth making a first foreign appointment. He succeeded in poaching Sven Goran Eriksson from Lazio: heedless of the fact that – as already discussed – Eriksson had not coached at national level. If Alf Ramsay had been inscrutable publicly, the low key, always infinitely polite Swede would emulate him, his emotions locked away: at least on the football field. His romantic liaisons were something else, their much-publicised details revealing a man possessed of galloping arousal, to the intermittent consternation of his employers.

Nevertheless, he led England to a spectacular victory in the return qualifier in Munich, England gleefully putting five goals past Germany, with a hat-trick from Michael Owen. It would need, however, a penalty from Beckham to rescue the team against Greece, in spite of which England headed for the finals in Japan/Korea high on optimism. Once more, expectation was to go unfulfilled. Sweden, Argentina and Nigeria were comfortably handled in the first round, Denmark in the second. A quarter final against Brazil then saw England founder, despite playing against ten men in the second half. A swirling free kick by Ronaldinho deceived a remorseful Seaman in goal, while Eriksson remained unmoving and seemingly unmoved on the bench, earning severe criticism back in his adopted home.

The same would be true at Euro '04 in Portugal. The coach once more showed tactical uncertainty on substitution in a quarter final against the hosts, England unluckily suffering the loss of an injured Wayne Rooney after half an hour, and going out on penalties. In the autumn of 2005, England's route to the finals of World Cup '06 fell on temporarily stony ground. Heavy defeat in a friendly against Denmark was followed by an unimpressive qualifying win over Wales, then humiliating defeat by lowly Northern Ireland in Belfast. Credibility was only rescued by a narrow victory at home over Austria, and then a more controlled performance against Poland. Media calls for Eriksson's dismissal had been running high. Nothing but a semi-final appearance in Germany the next summer, at worst, could now justify Eriksson's retention by the FA at £4 million a year. It was ironic that the victory over Poland in the final qualifying tie was achieved with Ledley King of Tottenham and Shaun Wright-Phillips, a recent expensive transfer from Manchester City to Chelsea, respectively replacing the iconic Steve Gerrard, injured, and David Beckham, suspended. Reliance by Eriksson upon the latter pair had seemed immovable. There was still much to do before Eriksson and his team could begin to approach the acclaim granted to those heroes of long ago.

Victory over Argentina in a friendly in the autumn of 2005, with two late goals from Michael Owen, gave England's ambitions a welcome up-beat note, though as Beckham would admit afterwards: 'This was a friendly, now we have to produce the same quality when it really matters'.

If Bobby Moore epitomised the authority of the team in 1966, from Bobby Charlton came the flair and the fantasy. It was Charlton, with his spectacular goals against Mexico in the first round and then Portugal in the semi-final, who lifted spectators from their seats when they had become dulled by Ramsey's expedient functionalism. If Moore brought pride, Charlton brought joy. There was a wonderful extravagance in his running, his side-step, and his lethal shooting from way out, that had been thrilling audiences world-wide ever since he first appeared as a teenager among Matt Busby's other Babes in 1956. If Moore was infinitely gratifying in his excellence, Charlton was intoxicating. Moore had said afterwards: 'That day, we had the world at our feet.' Bobby Charlton, too, looks back upon that victory as the best moment in a lifetime.

'What it did, I felt, was give everybody ideas, the feeling that anything is possible if you are professional about it. A feeling not to be afraid, that you have a chance to win *anything*. I think we were lucky that we had good players, although we've had some good players since then. I think we won because, like Alf, we knew we were the best [most efficient] team, though it's difficult when everyone criticises you all the time, as they did beforehand. Me, I thought my life would never be the same. No one could argue with what we'd done, it was a great achievement and now it was going to be difficult to push further, beyond that. It was the highlight of my whole career. When I first set off in football as a boy, I never even knew there was a World Cup. I just wanted to be a footballer. Winning the European Cup in 1968 with Manchester United can't compare. It's different. Winning the European Cup takes two years, you have to win the League first. The World Cup is a few weeks, and at the level of international football, you don't get away with mistakes.'

Charlton acknowledges, however, that maybe the style of England's victory under Ramsey had an adverse effect, in the long term, on the domestic front. 'I think it affected our game,' he reflects, 'because everyone now believed that the 4-3-3 formation, which we used, was the answer to everything, but many of the coaches and schoolmasters using it didn't know how to make it work. Bad players couldn't operate it, yet almost every club in the country changed to it almost immediately. I regret the fact, though I didn't realise it fully at the time, that the system led to the elimination of wingers. Previously, every club had two wingers. Suddenly, it was said, you didn't need them. Yet wing play is so exciting!'

Today, there is hardly a genuine English winger in the whole of the Premier League. There is Wright-Phillips, finally given a proper chance against Poland in October 2005 in the absence of a suspended Beckham and looking encouragingly dangerous, and a youthful Stewart Downing at Middlesborough. The rest, if one can properly call them wingers, are foreigners, primarily regarded as wide mid-fielders: Giggs of Wales and Ronaldo of Portugal with Manchester United, Ljungberg (Sweden) and Pires (France) with Arsenal, Robben (Holland) and Duff (Northern Ireland) with Chelsea. The game has indeed become so different from the way it was when I was young, playing on the wing for Cambridge University at Wembley and scoring a goal for Pegasus, twice Amateur Cup winners, against Queens Park at Hampden; then missing an open goal, on a bumpy pitch where the ball bobbled, for an England Amateur XI against Queens Park Rangers, that probably cost me a cap against Scotland a week later. That's football, of course. Yet then there was still the thrill, for players and spectators, of those huge triangles behind the full backs and stretching to the corner flags, where there was space to run, and to find the freedom from which to pull the ball back on to the feet or head of onrushing colleagues. Now the game is governed by defence, by money, by fear of failing. In winning the World Cup, Alf Ramsey helped bring England their greatest glory, but in doing so, inadvertently changed the face of the game. Perhaps for ever.

1

Difficult to Beat

ON WEDNESDAY, 6 July 1966 a Comet was approaching touch-down at London Airport. On board was the England football team, returning from Chorzow in Silesia where the previous day they had beaten Poland by the only goal at the conclusion of a preparatory four-match tour. The eighth World Cup for the Jules Rimet Trophy, for which England were the hosts, was to start in five days' time at Wembley. Jimmy Greaves, one of the best known of England's players, on account of his dazzling feats of goal-scoring for Chelsea as a youngster and subsequently for A.C. Milan and then Tottenham Hotspur, said in a loud voice with mock seriousness: 'I hope the pilot knows this landing is the only thing between England and winning the World Cup.' This moment of Cockney jest was not without justification. England, founders of the game more than a century before, were favourites not only with the London bookmakers, but with knowledgeable overseas observers because of their home advantage and also because, under the guidance of their team manager, Alf Ramsey, they had latterly been showing that consistency and coherence which would make them, if nothing else, exceedingly difficult to defeat. Greaves, the sporting world expected, was one of those who would be prominent in leading them towards triumph.

The mood of optimism ran right through the squad of twenty-two players, more especially among those who had reason to think they were established members of the team. Not that anyone's place was a sinecure under Ramsey's discerning, expedient selection, but a string of victories during the past seven months against Spain, West Germany, Scotland, Yugoslavia, Finland, Norway, Denmark and Poland had created a stability in which now no more than two or three positions were still open to argument in Ramsey's mind: whatever the habitual turbulence of public opinion which helps to make the game what it is. Just before the team had set out for Helsinki a relaxed Greaves, drawing on the pipe which had helped rid him of that nervous facial tic of younger days, had said reflectively: 'We could all be on the edge of virtual immortality as far as football's concerned. It's something you don't want to speak about. We're in with such a good chance it's unbelievable. I've argued with a lot of people, friends, and they don't give us any chance. But when you look at the last couple of years . . . '

The excitement, largely under-stated among players, was by no means confined to the English. Like many of the sixteen finalist countries, Brazil had been busy with preparatory matches. The champions of the last two tournaments, in Sweden and Chile, they had trounced Atlético Madrid in front of a 100,000 Spanish crowd which had been eager to see the incomparable Pelé. Such were his exploits, his almost magical technique for his club, Santos of São Paulo, and for Brazil since first astonishing the world as a seventeen-year-old in Sweden, it was true to say he had no equal. Because of Pelé, an otherwise now largely ageing Brazil was fancied as one of the main challengers to England as they attempted to win the trophy outright a third time. I had been to Madrid to interview Pelé for the *Sunday Telegraph*. Brown eyes dreamy under heavy lids, like a lion half asleep in the sun, he always had, off the pitch, a total relaxation. You would never guess he possessed, a mere five feet eight, the power once to have scored a goal from the half-way line. I had found him high with expectation for the coming weeks. 'You don't realise what this means to us in Brazil,' he said. 'We have more supporters going to England than went across the Andes to Chile. They are selling their cars to be able to say, "I was in England for the World Cup". No other nation would we trust to take our money for tickets in October and not receive the tickets till April.' The expectations were, sadly, to be soured. There would be aspects of this World Cup invoking comparisons with the fourteenth century, when Edward II had banned mob football for its unruliness.

England in May and June had contained the usual kind of sporting news which makes headlines, but which could not compare with the emotion and euphoria which was about to engulf the country. The *Daily Mail* had reported, on domestic soccer: 'Super League Near'. Times do not change. Ridgway and Blyth were half-way across the Atlantic in their rowing boat. Sheila Scott circumnavigated the globe in a single-engine plane in a record thirty-three days and three minutes. The popular former middleweight world-champion, Randolph Turpin, gave the final sad twist to his controversial life by shooting himself at the age of thirty-seven. Denis Law, one of the Scots deprived by the English League of taking part in the critical last qualifying match for his country against Italy in Naples the previous December, demanded £15,000 to re-sign for Manchester United; and promptly had his bluff called by Matt Busby, who put him on the transfer list, a move which soon restored him to his senses.

To the consternation of the Football Association, the Jules Rimet Trophy had been stolen while on display at an exhibition, and happily was found under a hedge by Pickles, a mongrel, who became an instant celebrity. When the World Cup took off, the English public had never encountered anything like it. Although the modestly re-developed stadiums at places such as Sunderland, Middlesbrough, Sheffield and Birmingham were less full than those of Lancashire and London, where Brazil and England were respectively playing, the television screen carried the tournament to almost every livingroom of the land. The first five matches covered live by the BBC were all in the top ten ratings, an unprecedented dominance for the institutional channel over its commercial rival. England's third match in the first round against France was viewed at home by more than thirty million. The final would have a global audience, exceptional in those days, of nearly five hundred million: yet the England players who won it were receiving a mere £60 a match, apart from an eventual and relatively modest bonus. Harold Wilson, the Labour Prime Minister, whose government was under severe international financial strain, flew home specially from Washington and would later claim, with that deft showman's mastery of the footlights, that the triumph was, of course, due at least in part to the current political administration!

On a Pullman restaurant car between London and Birmingham, a waiter, discussing the tournament with Denis Howell, the ubiquitous minister for sport, said: 'I haven't watched the game for years, but now I can't wait for the next match on television.' He was typical of the millions who were suddenly switched on, in every sense, to a sport which had the dramas, the goodies and baddies, which go to make up the day-to-day compulsive entertainment of the hugely popular soap operas. No one, it seemed, was immune. Ambassadors resident in the capital dictated memos that they would not be socially available between 7.30 and 9.30 p.m.; there were even flowers in the ladies' lavatory at Everton Football Club.

The progress of England's team, from a turgid beginning without goals against Uruguay to an exultant final victory against West Germany, with the satisfaction intensified by an abrupt necessity for extra time, was the stuff of fairy stories. Many of the pundits were, however, sceptical. For all the appeal of Bobby Charlton's brilliance, the team was not as effervescent as, say, Hungary, who only failed because they had no competent goalkeeper. Brazil crumbled, laid low by gerontophilia and some merciless tackling on Pelé, which characterised too much of the competition. The most extreme offenders in this were Argentina and Uruguay, who duly received the somewhat luke-warm wrath of FIFA, the world governing body, and later petulantly threatened to withdraw from future competitions.

The game was at a cross-roads, more than ever the victim of expediency in defensive tactics, legal and illegal, and the friction of differing interpretations, between races and continents, of the laws of the game: a friction which would continue and increase. England were themselves at the centre of this controversy of interpretation, possessing one of the most provocative of players in the demonic little Nobby Stiles, who was domestically part villain, part hero, and off the field the most pleasant and popular of figures.

The team was, by its own admission, unspectacular until the later stages; indeed it had had fluctuating fortunes for much of Ramsey's three and a half years in office. 'We weren't expected to win, by the public or most of the commentators,' reflects George Cohen, the right-back, who became a property developer in mid-Kent. Ray Wilson, his colleague at left-back who runs a small undertakers' business near Halifax, agrees: 'There were a lot of disbelievers at the start. We didn't go out to entertain, certainly, but the team had reached the co-ordination in which it could play comparatively poorly and still win. I'd always thought it was going to be difficult for the first three games. We scored few goals, but we didn't give much away. We were basically a defensive side. That was the first quality of the team . . . plus the ability and the willingness to *graft.*'

The team *did* have two or three exceptional players: the imperturbable Gordon Banks in goal; a central defender of rare perception in Bobby Moore, the captain; the intermittent explosiveness of the idolised Bobby Charlton, survivor of the Munich air crash. Yet what the team had above all, almost uniquely for a national as opposed to a club team, was a unity, a shared mental and physical harmony that was distinctive for its mutual respect between all members of the squad. Bobby Moore, whose premature death in 1994, aged fifty-one, saddened millions of admirers, recalled: 'There was a remarkable "togetherness". We took it for granted when we were part of the dressing-room then, and only realised its value later. That *buzz.* You suddenly notice it when it's not there.' It was the sort of togetherness, for instance, which a week before the start of the tournament saw

Jimmy Armfield, the right-back in the 1962 finals and now captain of the reserves, being carried off shoulder high following a runaway win over Arsenal at a deserted training ground in Hertfordshire. It was a togetherness, engendered by Ramsey, which would stay with them for the rest of their lives. 'When we had a reunion with many of the German team at Leeds to play a charity match for the Bradford disaster appeal,' Wilson says, 'there were players who were crying at the recollection of 1966.'

Bobby Charlton, who, through international celebrity and charity matches, and official functions with FIFA, has remained in touch with several of the German players, says: *'That* was the West German people's favourite team, even more in some ways than the '74 team which won the Cup. It's that team in England they remember. That's the match they want to talk about every time I go to Germany. There was something about it, and not just our disputed third goal. I always laugh, and tell them, "We'd have beaten you anyway!" Gordon Banks had almost nothing to do for most of the match. Our fourth goal was only one of a handful of chances we had in extra time.'

If the tournament ended on a dignified as well as an exciting note, that was in part due to the pervading attitude of Helmut Schoen, the German team manager. A gracious and generous man, who in a sixteen-year career at the head of Germany's football was to win more trophies than anyone in the game's history, he has been a signal example in his respect for the referee at all times. Living today in well-earned peaceful retirement with his long-patient wife, his flowers and dog and small covered swimming-pool and tranquil view of the surrounding Wiesbaden forests, he begrudges England nothing. 'It was wonderful to be in the final, to be at Wembley, which has such significance for foreigners. For us it was a huge success. We had done better than we had expected. We could go into the match feeling free, with nothing to lose. It was England who had more to lose. In the dressing-room afterwards our team was not on the bottom. The public had seen that our team could be a good loser.' Oh, that such an example might have proved infectious!

On a fine Monday evening, the Queen, smiling and tactfully dressed in neutral white, officially opened the competition before England kicked off against Uruguay. In those times of relaxed security, she stood unprotected in the centre of the pitch, and said: 'I welcome all our visitors and feel sure we shall be seeing some fine football.' She was to prove half right. Not only was the tournament to be disfigured by some ungainly fouling, but the entire tactical shape of the world game was undergoing a metamorphosis for which the England manager, as much and more than most, was fundamentally responsible. His was the gospel of functionalism. 'If you want me to pick teams to win unimportant matches, I will,' he had said in answer to criticism of his selections during the run of friendly matches in which England had been engaged in recent seasons, having as hosts not been required to qualify. 'An elaborate performance may not have been a good one,' he had said, implying a gulf between his requirements and the spectator's. It was a practical approach which bonded his players to him, and in turn his loyalty to them was unwavering, however lonely and rocky the path of public acceptance. 'He always lived within himself,' reflects Armfield, now a journalist and broadcaster after some years as a club team manager. 'I've not heard of one player who worked with him who ever had a bad word to say about Alf.' As Cohen says: 'Everyone *played* for him.'

They did indeed, but the spectacle was not to meet with universal acclaim. That respected French sports paper *L'Equipe* carried a cartoon during the later stages of the competition depicting Stiles as a vampire, with Bobby Charlton riding in a Rolls-Royce and the road being cleared of obstructing French and Argentinians by a servile referee. Where England possessed undoubted virtues, these were not immediately recognised, particularly by some of those who had been defeated. Schoen is more objective. 'I liked England's football, compared with most of the South Americans, but the best is a mixture. Brazil at one time had such a mixture, but they were always dependent on personalities to lift their morale. In the time of Pelé, they had superior tactics *and* the players.'

But not in 1966. The hosts, as throughout the history of the competition before and since, profited from a substantial home advantage. They played all their matches at Wembley – a further matter of controversy at the time – and their momentum was undoubtedly enhanced by the ever increasing emotion of their supporters, whose patriotism, in a nation as traditionally undemonstrative as the English, amounted almost to excess. Were the seeds of the Heysel disaster of the 1985 European Cup Final in Brussels at least partially sown nineteen years before? It was ironic that a German television commentator, Werner Schneider, should see fit to state: 'The English nationalism is more than football. Perhaps we learned our lesson because of the Second World War. Perhaps we think more than other people how mad this attitude is. You would expect it from countries who have nothing else . . . but in England, it is strange and sad. They want to fly flags and beat drums because they are winning at football. It is said that the Germans are the most militaristic people, but this is not so. The British are. Even winning at football is treated like winning a battle.'

Those who experienced the nationalism of West German

supporters in their own country in 1974, not to mention the fanaticism of Argentinians in the streets and stadiums in 1978 in Buenos Aires, or indeed the Mexicans in 1970 (and all too predictably again in 1986), may consider Herr Schneider's views somewhat hypocritical. Yet it is not to be denied that, with the aid of television's communication, and the deliberate elevation of nationalism, as opposed to football quality, in the process of the World Cup's qualifying competition, the fires of emotional reaction to a simple game have been grossly encouraged. Mounting materialism, growing side by side with extreme social stresses in almost all countries, has made football the excuse as well as a safety valve for pent-up aggression among spectators. There may well be a difference between the emotions of national unity, echoing the team's success, fostered among ordinary people in 1966, and the disgraceful, rampant minority draped in Union Jacks who over the next twenty years went pillaging in foreign cities in drunken disorder to the point where the English were belatedly banned. But the connection, I believe, was there: the vicarious fulfilment in sporting success which encouraged the unthinking to see failure as intolerable and to interpret success as a material substitute instead of an abstract.

It is here worth reproducing from a percipient, and unheeded, article by Edward Grayson, a barrister and authority on sport and the law (and the author of *Corinthians and Cricketers)*, which was published in the *FA Year Book, 1967–68:*

The explosion surrounding the dismissal of Rattin, the Argentine captain, by Herr Kreitlein, at Wembley Stadium, illuminated the problems of international football law and its interpretation at flashpoint level. The anger which raged throughout the international football world, especially the threatened breakaway by the South American footballing nations from FIFA, symbolised the wider international problem. An awareness of the parallel anxieties in international legal circles would have allayed many of the fears felt at that time for the future wellbeing of international football. Indeed, the question which inevitably follows every World Cup Competition, of how the differing constructions of the Laws of the Game can be harmonised within the framework of their 17 different statutory provisions, diverts attention from one simple yet crucial factor which many tend to ignore or overlook. It is that while general international affairs and law grope painfully towards a Utopian yet unreal ideal, international football has become a dynamic reality based upon the English-made Laws of the Game which the domestic British pastime has taken to the four corners of the globe.

This reality was rationalised into an international framework by the creation of FIFA in 1904 and the existence today of the International Football Board on which the early law-makers from Britain and representatives from the rest of the world, which accepted the Laws, are equally balanced. Whatever the faults of international football, and every institution operated by human beings possesses them, at least it works for the general benefit of mankind. When it creates conflicts and tensions, these are reflected in a wider and more sophisticated international sphere.

In this perspective, football as an international game and art form must mirror in its sensitivity the social environment surrounding it, just as Sir Neville Cardus has maintained throughout that the English summer game has always responded to the mood and tempo of the social climate of any particular period. Correspondingly, the problems which beset football generally are inevitably the problems which beset society generally. To isolate the ills which afflict the game at any particular period from the sickness suffered by society at the same time does the game a disservice and demonstrates a superficial and myopic naivety . . .

In an age of violence, the question of punishments and penalties produces even greater problems than policing the laws to be observed, and in this setting the development of violence on and off the field of play and how to control it is a symptom of a wider ailment. This problem of control is no different at international or domestic football levels. They are inter-related by the difficulties of constructing the Laws of the Game in a split second, in particular Law 12 dealing with penal offences. The difficulties of timing a decision are no different from those of policemen who exercise their power of arrest, with the exception that the policemen are professional officers of the law. In football the policing of the field of play is in the hands of semi-professionals or amateurs who also are obliged to carry out the role of timekeepers, goal judges, adjudicators, and courts of appeal! . . .

What should not be evaded much longer is the separate problem of enforcing law and order off the field of play with penalties commensurate with offences which take place on it. A FIFA Committee issued edicts before, during and after the World Cup Competition of 1966; but it could not prevent the curtailment in the tournament of the participation of the outstanding player, Pelé of Brazil. The Inter-Cities Fairs Cup Committee took disciplinary action against Roma following incidents in their game against Chelsea. But hooliganism is still rampant on too many terraces, and though star players at all levels, professional and amateur, are suspended and fined, the thuggery of the minority still spoils the game as a pastime, as a profession, and as a spectacle for the majority. No profundity is required to note that violence on the field is related to terrorism off it, and vice versa. Yet however overworked and sometimes too merciful are FA Disciplinary Committees at domestic level, the offences continue and the image of the game is further tarnished. The increase of crime throughout the land in no way diminishes the disrepute into which football in England is dragged by the acts of its criminals on and off the field of play . . . .

What is now required at all levels of the game is an awareness that those who break the laws of football on the field and the laws of society off it should be branded equally as criminals and wrong-doers. The player who commits a foul can maim an opponent for life and deprive him of his livelihood; a grave foul can kill. If the players and the clubs will not control the lawlessness which besmirches the game's good name, then it could yet be controlled for them. The motor car emerged as a potential benefit to mankind: it became a potential killer. The law accordingly developed until, by common sense, three offences were made the limit for automatic disqualification. If the present range of football crime on and off the field continues unchecked then the whole range of penalties will require careful re-examination. If the authorities will make the punishment fit the crime, if the clubs will join hands with the forces of law and order and let it be known that offending players and spectators will not be tolerated; and if the players and spectators will themselves look around them and condemn the law-breaker, then the game which has created a more universally accepted and effective international law than any other sphere of international society can yet give a lead to restoring order to the lives of the majority. In this way football at both the international and domestic level will not only reflect society: it will be ahead of it.

All too regrettably, football authorities have glaringly lacked such wisdom, consumed as much as the players with material greed. Any dignified sport would have suspended for life the West German goalkeeper for his atrocious foul in the 1982 semi-final, which shamefully handicapped the French. From FIFA there was no more than a murmur.

The period of 1966 was not without its other, unheeded, lessons. Shortly before the finals began, Arsenal had their lowest attendance, 4,554, since Highbury was opened in 1913, when losing 3-0 at home to Leeds on the same night that there was a live television broadcast of the European Cup Winners final at Hampden Park, Glasgow, in which Borussia Dortmund defeated Liverpool. That was the moment for the football authorities to recognise the true threat of television: thirty years later they still have not, and it is too late. They have become semi-dependent on the parasites. The television income in the Premiership, and from the Champions League, has created a coterie of super-rich clubs and obscenely over-paid players, but the gravy-train may yet run dry.

Yet this story is about England's winning of the World Cup. After they had done it, George Raynor, a wise old English coach from Yorkshire, unheralded at home and responsible for guiding Sweden to the 1958 final against Brazil, had observed: 'There is in football no substitute for skill . . . but the manager's job is usually to try to find one. Ramsey obviously found one.' Was Raynor fair?

2

Was Walter Unlucky?

'**O**F COURSE, I suppose *you* will be staying till the end.' This remark, which I had from a member of the England squad before the quarter-final against Brazil during the World Cup in Chile in 1962, epitomised the somewhat defeatist attitude at that time of too many of those who represented England. Such was England's record, having won only two matches away from home against front-rank opposition in four final competitions, that to be defeated by Brazil now seemed to some to be the ultimate honour. 'We had no mental attitude for playing abroad at that time,' says Bobby Charlton, who had then already played for England for five seasons. 'We never seemed to go anywhere that mattered and *win*. There were too many team changes. People played once, and were never seen again. Maybe that was the selection committee, not the manager. Teams were mostly selected on Monday. If you'd scored a hat-trick on Saturday, you were in! That's nonsense.'

It was indeed the fault of the selectors. A body of eight or nine well-intentioned, but predominantly ill-informed men would randomly roam the country surveying league matches, on the chance prospect of being in the right place when something notable happened. A hat-trick was about all that most of them were equipped to recognise, for seldom did they have any real experience, even as former amateur players. Graham Doggart, chairman of the FA at this time and a former Corinthian of some merit, was a comparatively rare exception. 'I can remember a conversation with one of the selectors in Chile,' John Connelly reminisces, 'and all the time it was Alan this and Alan that. He thought I was our reserve goalkeeper, Alan Hodgkinson.' Connelly, who with his wife runs a busy fish restaurant near Nelson in Lancashire, did not get a game in Chile, being deputy for that weaving Blackburn winger Bryan Douglas: Connelly would be in the squad again four years later.

Walter Winterbottom, who had paid his way through Carnegie College of Physical Education with his modest wages as an unspectacular Thirties professional at Old Trafford, combined the functions of England team manager and director of coaching. He was in charge for fifteen years at a period of England's most colourful football. Yet it was a period in which reputation, partially a hang-over from pre-war dominance, had begun, especially by the Fifties, not to be justified by performance and results. Europe and some Latin American countries had begun rapidly overhauling the former masters. This shift in power had been early detected by Sir Stanley Rous, for nearly thirty years the FA secretary, and by Winterbottom himself. Yet though Winterbottom established a school of coaching and ideas, from which emanated a string of young professionals who would become the intelligent team managers of tomorrow, Walter himself too often found that England fell short.

There was the shock defeat by the United States, in the 1950 World Cup at Belo Horizonte in Brazil, of a team containing some of the most illustrious names in England's football history: Ramsey, Wright, Dickinson, Finney, Mannion and Mortensen – Matthews only playing in the subsequent match, a defeat by Spain. There had been little preparation or organisation for the venture and, having lost, England immediately returned home without leaving behind anyone to observe the progress of their rivals.

At home, the defeat received no more than a few paragraphs' notice: English football continued its way with the majority of the public and football officials in blissful ignorance. Tom Finney says: 'There wasn't much planning in those days. We met about a week before at Roehampton and flew out two or three days before the start. We were playing at the game like an amateur side. There was no tactical planning for any of the matches. Walter was a great theorist, going through the opposition, but discussing them as individuals and not as a team. I cannot remember a single occasion on which he said how we were to play tactically.' It was little different four years later in Switzerland. Prior to the 1954 World Cup, the truth had been finally driven home by the thirteen goals England had conceded home and away to Hungary. With the selectors making no fewer than forty-four team and positional changes in the ten matches that season, it was little surprise when England – Finney, Matthews and all – were swept away in the World Cup by lowly Switzerland and talented Uruguay.

To be fair to Winterbottom, although he was at the mercy of his fluctuating selectors he did manage to persuade them, for almost the entire period of his management, to maintain a consistent defensive six: goalkeeper, two full-backs, and three half-backs in the old 'WM' formation. For those too young to recall, that formation had remained more or less standard from the time of the change in the off-side law in the Twenties to the late Fifties: a defensive centre-half operating between rotating full-backs (the 'free' full-back giving cover when the ball was on the other flank), the wing-halves operating a midfield quartet with deep-lying inside-forwards behind a front trio of centre-forward and two wingers. The WM was a 3-4-3 formation. An increasing tendency for one of the wing-halves to be more defensive and one of the inside-forwards to lie upfield in support of his centre-forward eventually became formalised, notably by Brazil and then emulated by England and others, as a 4-2-4 formation. Hungary, under the guidance of Gustav Sebes, had maintained a more attacking 3-3-4 formation.

In 1950, Winterbottom's back six – the W – had been Williams, Ramsey, Aston, Wright, Franklin (until he defected to Columbia) and Dickinson. By 1954, with Wright switching to centre-half, it had become Merrick, Staniforth, Roger Byrne, McGarry, Wright and Dickinson. By 1956-57 this had become Hopkinson, Howe, Byrne, Clayton, Wright and Edwards, while a consistent forward line had begun to emerge of Douglas (at last displacing Matthews), Kevan or Bobby Robson, Tommy Taylor, Haynes and Finney. There is no doubt that with this formation, which had scored an exceptional sixty-one goals in twenty-one matches with only three defeats, and with such brilliant youngsters as Charlton and Pegg of Manchester United standing eagerly in the wings, Winterbottom had the makings of a team with genuine credentials for winning the 1958 World Cup in Sweden. Such hopes were shattered by Manchester United's air crash in February 1958, in which Byrne, Edwards, Taylor and Pegg all died. The twenty-year-old Charlton survived, made his debut against Scotland, still in a state of shock, two months later; was dropped from the team for the World Cup in Sweden, and did not re-establish himself until the following season.

In Sweden, England nevertheless drew all their first-round matches, with the Soviet Union, Brazil and Austria, all among the toughest opposition then available. They were the only team in the finals against whom the rampant Brazilians failed to score; but in a play-off for a place in the quarter-final, they lost to the Soviet Union by the only goal. Eight years on from Belo Horizonte, the administration still made inadequate concessions to the requirements of the team. The hotel was in the busy centre of Gothenburg, and for all the team's adequate performances there was a slight schism between players and manager. 'I can remember us all going to a swimming-pool,' Bobby Charlton says. 'Walter went down the slide, causing a great splash. I jokingly called out "Good old Walter", and there was a silence all round, with the older players staring at me. You weren't supposed to make fun of the manager. I remember when I first played, against Scotland, a few weeks before. I suppose they thought I would be nervous, so they put me in a room with Billy [Wright]. He was a nice fellow, but he didn't have much influence as a captain. There was such a turnover of players that I think he was reluctant to criticise anything, in case anyone thought it was his fault if they were dropped.'

By the time Winterbottom arrived in Chile, he again had a comparatively settled team and possibly his most impressive sequence of results ever. The regular team was: Springett; Armfield and Wilson; Robson, Swan or Norman, and Flowers; Douglas or Connelly, Greaves, Haynes and Charlton, with a doubt only about centre-forward, which had varied between Bobby Smith, Hitchens, Pointer, Crawford and Peacock. In the final match before arriving in Chile, Greaves scored a hat-trick in a 4-0 defeat of Peru in Lima, where Bobby Moore made his debut as a replacement for the injured Robson.

A realistic analysis of the capabilities of the England team, with three forwards and two full-backs of outstanding international quality, suggested that if they applied themselves they need be inferior to none, including Brazil. Yet the lack of collective will, to which Charlton has referred, was quickly to undermine morale at the training camp at Coya, in the hills above Rancagua, where they would play their first-round matches. The facilities were provided by the American-owned Braden Copper Company, at their settlement some 2,500 feet up in the Andes and an hour's ride from Rancagua. This was regarded as ideal, following the dissatisfaction in Gothenburg. The players occupied three large bungalows, taking meals in a communal dining-room supervised by an English cook; with training on an adjacent pitch, the ready use of a golf course close by, a cinema, a bowling alley, and tennis courts. True professionals setting out on the most ambitious project of their career should have found such circumstances perfect. However, there were cliques within the squad, and discontent soon set in at the remoteness of this wonderfully healthy location. The opening match against Hungary was lost 2-1, some of the players already pining for home. Lajos Baroti, that marvellously sporting manager of Hungary, slightly took Winterbottom's breath away when he caught his arm just before the start and wished him good luck; but an ill at ease England team, seldom pulling together, needed more than luck and went down to goals by Tichy and Albert.

Winning the next match against Argentina 3-1 and then drawing drably with Bulgaria, England qualified for a quarter-final with Brazil: an unconvincing side playing without real heart. Back in the dressing-room after playing Bulgaria, there was a row between Charlton and Haynes, who had claimed, 'Well, we've made it.' Charlton was angry. 'I told him we'd not frightened anyone, not shown people what we *really* might do. Some of the lads were wanting to get home and there was even talk that one of them would be cheering for Brazil. We had a very good side that became delapidated. I'd really thought we'd win the World Cup in Chile, which was what made me so confident for the next time. In that quarter-final, I think we could have won, but for Garrincha. He was beating anyone and everybody. Pelé, who had been injured, was replaced by an unknown called Amarildo, who was so good he could play one-twos off the cross-bar! Maybe we would have lost to them anyway.'

Throughout the four matches neither Greaves nor Haynes approached the limit of his ability, though Greaves had a good first half against Argentina. There was some feeling that the famous pair might have been replaced by Hunt and Eastham. Hunt, hugely consistent, was a corner stone of the powerful Liverpool team while Eastham, the player who had challenged the legality of the transfer system in his move from Newcastle to Arsenal, was an outstanding figure in the Under 23 team. It was, of course, most improbable that Winterbottom would have replaced Haynes, his captain, other than because of injury. I had personally played against Haynes ten years earlier when he was a member of the FA Youth XI, and was well aware of his extreme perception as a passer of the ball. In the opinion of Cohen, his colleague at Fulham, Haynes was 'the greatest foot-to-ball player I have ever seen.' Yet the responsibility invested in Haynes by the 4-2-4 system which England were now playing, and increased by the replacement of Robson as his midfield partner by the then inexperienced Moore, was too great a load. Haynes, under the pressures of a World Cup, tended too much to chastise his colleagues for their occasional inadequacies; and there is the lasting memory of this accomplished player rebuking a colleague who had lost the ball immediately prior to Hungary's first goal, when Haynes himself had the scope to close down the advancing opponent.

There were precedents on hand for famous players being dropped: Spain left out Suarez and Del Sol after losing to Czechoslovakia, nearly eliminating Brazil, against whom they were leading until late in the game. Armfield is even more emphatic than Charlton about the quarter-final. 'We could have won against Brazil, I am convinced, in the right frame of mind.

We missed some sitters.' An English resident, asked what Greaves had done against Brazil, replied caustically that he had caught a stray dog during an interruption. There were some members of the side not prepared to accept that when you lose a match you should have to crawl off the pitch, not walk off. A senior player said before England flew home: 'Some of our fellows didn't have the guts or the dedication.'

Moore said that he did not have clear recollections of Chile; that he was somewhat overawed to find himself in the same company as Haynes, whom only that season he had been to watch as a spectator at Wembley. Greaves, with his disarming frankness and nonchalance, admits: 'We blew it. You remember what it was like . . . You couldn't explain the circumstances to a team today, crowds of only two or three thousand at the early games. It was all a horror. Had we stayed at Vasco da Gama, where we were for the quarter-final, we might have done better.'

In no sense attempting to shift the blame from the players to the manager, Greaves none the less pin-points one part of the difference between the mood then and that which would be established during the coming year. 'It was much more cavalier, more fun with Walter, a more relaxed atmosphere. Things changed with Alf. He told the selectors to get lost, and it became a more professional outfit. Walter was a joy, although I never understood a word he said. He came out with some marvellous phrases. I used to think what on earth is he talking about, but I loved him all the same. I had the same respect for Alf, but the fun *did* go out of it. You could argue about who had the better team. Banks was probably better than Springett, but I would say Armfield was better than Cohen, and they're both mates. Jack [Charlton] will shoot me, but I would say Swan was the better centre-half. And the forward line? Douglas, self, Smith, Haynes, Charlton. Bloody hell, that was some front line, or at any rate *I* thought it was. So did the Scots! You can argue whether Moore was better than Flowers, too . . . ? The thing about Walter was he could smile quite easily in defeat. If I wanted a manager who'd make friends, it would be Walter. If I wanted a winning team I'd take Alf. He brought atmosphere and spirit. This was something Walter failed to do. Too often during Walter's era, teams were like strangers, on and off the pitch.'

The difference between Winterbottom and Ramsey, in Wilson's opinion, was Ramsey's total professionalism. 'Walter was more an ambassador. How could Alf fail with all those good players, after what he'd achieved at Ipswich? I talked about it with Bobby Charlton at the time. He said Manchester United had had ninety per cent of the ball and were always in Ipswich's half of the field and they still lost – and he was left scratching his head. As far as nerves go, I much preferred playing in Chile to playing at Wembley four years later. The tension was immense. I really felt for the Spanish team playing at home in '82. They looked like a non-league side. They were paralysed by anxiety.'

Bobby Charlton is probably the most accurate thermometer of the two eras, because he was the least like the alleged 'Ramsey style' of player. He experienced enough of both men to be objective. 'Walter didn't criticise you individually. If you played badly, you wouldn't know until the next team was picked and you weren't in it. There was no feeling of *belonging* in the team. Walter had this impeccable accent, whereas football's a poor man's game, players expect to be sworn at . . . a bit of industrial language. Through no fault of his own, Walter used to make it seem an academic language. Walter used to go through things in discussion that I felt were obvious to people who were supposed to be good players. It was theory all the time. What made things difficult was that you never played more than a couple of matches with the same players. Haynes was the only one who never was altered. He was always shouting, forceful. If someone gave a bad pass, he'd bawl at them. He didn't seem to realise that attacking the player didn't help. We'd always had a good record at home. Teams never used to come to England and win, so I knew it would be difficult for them in '66. In '62, I wasn't confident in the system, but when Alf came there was continuity, no longer the turnover of players. There were people who came in with Alf who would never have been there with Walter: Nobby Stiles, maybe Jack, Hunt, even though he had a scoring record. Walter's idea of a midfield man was that he had to be attack-minded, but the professional view had become that you had to have someone to win the ball. Nobby had a questionable reputation, but that meant nothing to Alf, it was the job he needed. *I* couldn't win the ball, so I depended on Nobby and Ray Wilson to give it to me.'

Winterbottom was candid about the shifts in emphasis in the game, highlighted first by the Austrians and then by Hungary, which had helped put his conventional style out of date. 'We hadn't seen the way continental teams were developing blind-side runs off the ball. We were open and straightforward, playing to our established system.' Following the disappointment of Chile, there was a public clamour for Winterbottom's replacement by a professional coach with exclusive power of selection as was now common to most foreign teams. Winterbottom, ousted in his attempt to switch to succeed Rous as secretary of the FA and later knighted for services to sport following a period as director of the Sports Council, is now in retirement. He reflected: 'In 1962, I was reaching an age when I felt I couldn't continue being an active coach, when players no longer take you seriously. I recommended to Graham Doggart that he should try to get Jimmy Adamson from Burnley, an outstanding young coach, but Jimmy didn't want to move from the north. It was a pity, I thought he had a great career in front of him.' Thus ended Winterbottom's distinguished era as manager, during which time England had played 137 matches and had won 78, drawn 32 and lost 27. The measure of their disparity home and away was that of those 27 defeats only two had been to foreigners at home: Hungary in 1953 and Sweden in 1959. His teams had not travelled well, though he himself had become one of the most respected of men in the international field. It was an act of astonishing and self-destructive pettiness, comparable to ignoring Moore's potential as a global ambassador, when the intellectual dwarfs of the FA threw out his experience as potential General-secretary two months later, electing instead Dennis Follows, a rugby follower who was secretary of the Airline Pilots' Association.

3

The Coming of Ramsey

Late in february, 1963, England were to play a second qualifying leg of the European Championship – then called the Nations Cup – in Paris. The previous autumn, between the resignation of Winterbottom and the appointment of Ramsey, the first leg had been played at Hillsborough, resulting in a dull two-goal draw. Only Greaves of the World Cup attack played: Haynes and Charlton were injured, and the selectors in one of their last flings before conceding selection to the new manager sent out a hotch-potch of four new caps, bestowing another three in attack for the subsequent 3-1 win over Northern Ireland, two more when beating Wales. By the time the return came against France, the quiet man from Ipswich had taken charge, though too late for selecting the squad. When they gathered at Hendon Hall Hotel prior to departure, Ramsey met the squad for the first time. 'Just call me Alf,' he said in a simple, brief chat, putting the players at their ease. A new era had begun.

Not that it began too well. England were thumped 5-2, Henry of Spurs at left-back proving vulnerable to the pace and changes of direction of Wisnieski, a brilliant winger who had been a star of the 1958 semi-final team. The official *FA Year Book* for 1963-64 made no mention of Ramsey's appointment in its report of the match, nor in its editorial by the new secretary, Denis Follows. It did contain a profile of Major Jack Stewart, the vice-chairman, just as the previous season's *Year Book* had a profile of the new secretary. The only way the otherwise uninformed reader might have known that a major change of policy had taken place in the FA's most public area of activity was from the small photograph of the team beaten 2-1 in Scotland, which included in the back row 'A. Ramsey, manager'. It was for some years to be a cool relationship between the lone professional in his small, insignificant office at Lancaster Gate and the profusion of committees of power-wielding amateur councillors. It was an entirely different relationship to that immediately established with the players. 'He's a good bloke, Alf,' Bobby Charlton was soon disposed to say. 'He never varies one way or the other, win or lose. You always know where you are with him.'

Ramsey was born on 22 January 1920, though for some while during his playing career he tended to hedge about the date. With his career delayed by the war, he came somewhat late to the game, and as a full-back not over-endowed with speed his age was likely to be viewed in those conventional times as a measure of his potential: therefore the calculated uncertainty. The date was reported variously in different publications, and it was only ultimately to *Debrett's Peerage* that he eventually gave the correct date.

Ramsey's father was a hay and straw dealer with a small-holding in Dagenham, that flat anonymous area of southern Essex. Playing for Southampton as an amateur while on army service, Ramsey turned professional for them as a reserve, receiving eight pounds a week if he played for the first team, in 1944. He was then a centre-forward, but was converted by Bill Dodgin, the manager, to full-back. From the earliest stage of his career, the young player, quiet and reserved, showed himself to be painstaking at practising to improve his ball control, his passing, kicking, penalty taking . . . and his speech. The accent of Dagenham he seemingly found disadvantageous, and discreet elocution lessons produced a careful but somewhat mannered diction that would often be undermined by too elaborate phrases. Able to identify instantly with his players, in an emotional way which had always eluded Winterbottom, Ramsey never acquired Winterbottom's ease in public company. During the next ten years this short-coming, which he had commendably sought to eliminate, was to prove a major deficiency in his public relations. It was a pity, for he was a studious reader of serious books, and an outstanding thinker of the game.

One of his virtues was that, unlike so many professionals, he profited from almost every experience. Arriving at a London hotel for his first international match, away to Italy in Turin, he was not at first recognised by the established players such as Swift, Wright and Lawton, and was obliged to introduce himself. He would not forget this. He would remember, too, that it was England's superior fitness, enabling them to outlast the technically clever Italians, that made a major contribution to their 4-0 victory.

His first cap came the following season, 1948-49, in the 6-0 victory over Switzerland, and he surprised his room-mate, Jackie Milburn of Newcastle, by sitting up half the night talking tactics, something almost unknown at such time. He raised some eyebrows, too, by occasionally ordering the maestro on the right-wing to: '*Hold* it!!' There were not many, least of all full-backs, who attempted to tell Matthews how to play. The following year, at the advanced age of twenty-nine, he signed for Spurs for a transfer fee of £21,000, immediately finding an inspirational environment under the caring intelligence of Arthur Rowe, the Tottenham manager. Rowe, whose wisdom I had the good fortune to experience during his several years as coach to Pegasus after ill health forced him to retire at White Hart Lane, recalls that Ramsey was always talking, always thinking, challenging ideas before accepting them. He was one of the first to raise the importance for a marker of watching the man and not the ball.

My first experience of professional football was as a fifteen-year-old, attending a coaching course in London – under the direction of Walter – and taking myself one spring evening to Fulham to watch them play Spurs. I was mesmerised, not so much by Baily and Duquemin and Medley, as by this remarkable fellow at right-back, who played football in a way I had never supposed a defender to be capable. In those days, full-backs tended to be players you heard coming a long way off, like horses. Ramsey was a revelation. His skill made no difference, regrettably, when the USA defeated England in the World Cup. Helping Spurs to win the Second Division and the League Championship in successive seasons, it was Ramsey who for the next couple of years helped preserve England's now porous reputation. Personally fascinated by the devastating passwork and positioning of Austria and by their attacking half-back Ocwirk, Ramsey calmly scored the penalty which saved England from defeat; and he did so again in 1953 when, with a minute to go, they were 4-3 down in the 90th anniversary match against a superb FIFA XI. Then, at the age of thirty-four, in the last of his thirty-two appearances, he was among those overwhelmed in England's first home defeat, 6-3 by Hungary. Ramsey, mentally as stubborn as ever, insisted: 'We should never have lost.'

Two seasons later Ramsey was on the move again, accepting the opportunity of becoming manager with the modest little East Anglian club, Ipswich, in the Third Division South. At that time the Ipswich secretary was still a crusty old-stager, Scott Duncan, who held many of the administrative strings and gave the new young manager a difficult time. Several times in his first season Ramsey is said to have given in his notice, but John Cobbold, the club's affably eccentric and aristocratic chairman, jocularly told his young manager to go away 'and grow some more skin'. When Duncan retired, Ramsey insisted on being secretary-manager, and on being involved in every aspect of the club's administration right down to choosing the grass seed. After two seasons Ipswich won promotion to the Second Division, and there are those who can remember a cheerful and unwinding Ramsey, seated informally on the floor at a celebration and heartily singing 'Maybe it's because I'm a Londoner'. Those who came to know him socially over the coming years discovered that in the later hours of the evening, after a glass or two, Alf could become engaging company. At work, he so often seemed remote. 'How about that!' exclaimed Cobbold, emotionally jabbing his manager in the ribs as an opposing defender put the ball in his own net one winter evening. 'It's cold, isn't it?' said a dead-pan Ramsey.

Winterbottom had, of course, seen plenty of Ramsey as a player, and had been able to observe his character. 'He was exceedingly sensitive and found it difficult to take any kind of personal remark. Once, I remember, some official of the Sports Council made a fairly inoffensive point about the England team, when Alf was manager, as a conversation opener at a dinner and Alf was upset and taut for the rest of the evening. Yet he could keep cool when everyone around him was disintegrating. That was why he was such a good penalty taker. He was extremely quiet, set apart from other players a bit, but good-natured. I remember him starting to take an interest in coaching, so I invited him to come down with me on one occasion to Winchester School, to get the feel of what was involved. He did outstandingly well, but never took the full badge of our coaching course, and went to Ipswich before he had had time. I don't know whether he was one of those professionals who have difficulty getting over the embarrassment of being good players but needing to be taught how to coach. I never saw him perform later as a coach but he was one of the thinkers of the game. He would always come up with some original aspect. He was a nice man, but it was hard to know how to get at him. He *loved* football. He was calculating, fair and honest as a full-back, concentrating his skill on distribution. He was a players' player.'

The ultimate such players' player was a skinny, nondescript Scot around whom Ramsey built an innovative tactical system for Ipswich, like Tottenham, to win the Second Division and League Championship in successive seasons, in 1961-62: Jimmy Leadbetter. Several years before anyone had become aware of the overseas adaptation, Ramsey devised a flexible 4-4-2 formation in which his wingers, Leadbetter and Stephenson, played mostly wide in midfield. Opposing full-backs were put in a dilemma: whether to go with the wingers, thereby leaving gaps behind in their defence, or whether to stand off and allow Ipswich possession. Up front, Ramsey had Phillips, a tall, angular inside-forward who could whack the ball like a mule's hind kick; and

Crawford, one of the new breed of scheming centre-forwards who could play facing the wrong way, with his back to the defence, and was able to control the ball and lay it off to colleagues when it was played up to him . . . as often as not by Leadbetter. In the promotion year, Crawford and Phillips scored a remarkable 33 and 28 goals respectively. Crawford, while Winterbottom was still England manager, gained Ipswich's first international caps, against Ireland and Austria in 1961-62. The key to Ipswich's historic league title in 1962, which made Ramsey's name and prevented Spurs doing the double, were their home and away victories over Tottenham, including an encounter at Easter at the peak period of Tottenham's semi-finals in the FA Cup against Manchester United and European Cup against Benfica.

Yet by October 1962, in their second season in the First Division, Ipswich were already exposed and in trouble, third from bottom in the table. The opposition, now wise to the Ipswich system, had adjusted their tactics, using midfield players and not full-backs to mark Leadbetter and Stephenson and closing down the spaces which Crawford and Phillips had previously exploited. However, this did not concern the FA who, rejected by Adamson, were glad to appoint the champion manager. Ramsey's former England room-mate, Milburn, took on the task of saving an Ipswich club seriously short of reserve and youth material; steered them clear for one season but could not prevent them going down the next year.

There are those who say that Ramsey bequeathed Milburn a stricken ship, that he himself would not have been able to prevent the drift back into anonymity. Yet he was about to confirm, in an even more exposed field, his ability to find the right formula using unexpected elements. 'We knew even before he became England manager there must be something special about him,' Cohen says. 'When you looked at Ipswich's title, you had to ask how could it possibly happen? It *had* to be down to the manager. I remember the year they won it, we beat them 10-0 at the Cottage. I was marking Jimmy Leadbetter. Four days later we went to Ipswich and lost 4-2! After twenty minutes, I was nowhere near Leadbetter, I didn't know where to go. Graham Leggat said, "Get on the half-way line," but I decided to try and mark a zone, which is what we should all have done in the first place. What was impressive about Alf when he took charge of the England squad was that there was no player who was bigger than him, unlike Haynes with Winterbottom, or Keegan with Revie and Greenwood. He was strong on discipline, but it was subtle. He *advised* you to go to bed early. He never demanded. But when he said, "I'd like you to be in by such and such a time," it was like paying the rates. You couldn't avoid it. He was a terribly kind person, and thoughtful, and he could have a dry wit. It was easy to like him. He was fond of his jellied eels and brown ale.'

Yet, however close the players were to him, there was nevertheless always a certain distance. 'You could never weigh him up, never reckon him,' John Connelly says. 'Yet I wished I could have played under him with a club. He brought the best out of you. He had a gentle way of getting at you. Once, when the ball ran out when we were playing at Hampden, I went and fetched it and threw it to a Scot. They took a quick throw, went down the line and damn near scored. Watching the video afterwards, Alf said to the rest of the lads, "Just watch this pillock. What do you think of that, running after the effing ball for an effing Scotsman!"'

Not long after his appointment, Ramsey inadvertently made a rod for his own back for the next three years. In an interview with a local journalist in Ipswich, subsequently reported round the world, Ramsey stated that England would win the World Cup. Being Alf, and having thought about it, there was no qualification. That was his emphatic way: not boastful, but sure. On his first summer tour with the squad he would start to provide the evidence. In an unparalleled sequence, for England, of away victories, Czechoslovakia were beaten 4-2, East Germany 2-1 and Switzerland 8-1. Into the side had come Banks, Milne in midfield with Moore moving to centre-back, Eastham and Paine. There were many instances on this formative trip of his insistence on the team ethic. After the first win in Bratislava, Greaves asked in the evening if he might go and have a drink at the bar. 'If you want a drink, you can have it here with us,' said Ramsey.

Charlton at this stage was still playing on the left wing, in which position he had been voted the outstanding player by the international press the previous year in Chile. 'The most fundamental difference between him and Walter was that Alf talked about the game like a real club pro,' Charlton says. 'He'd been one. He never said an opponent was good unless he was. He was difficult to approach with opinions, but that was probably right. The players *don't* know best. Alf was never influenced by any player. He was always after what made a team rather than individuals. If he was going to be hung, it would be on his decision. I've seen players influence managers before and since on the way of playing, and it's not healthy. He made you feel you were picked because you were a good player, and he talked about what *you* needed. In Bratislava, he made me train in the area of the pitch where I would be playing, try the corner kicks to get the feel of the run-up. He was meticulous. Yet although I respected and liked him, I don't know anyone who actually *knew* him. He could be obstinate. You couldn't shift him. When we once asked why we always stayed at Hendon Hall in London, with so much travelling to Roehampton for training, he simply said, "We stay at Hendon because it's near Wembley." It was a waste of time arguing.'

In the spring of 1964, England were to play a friendly in Portugal, gathering first, as always, at Hendon. The evening before travelling, Moore, Charlton, Wilson, Banks, Eastham, Johnny Byrne and Hunt broke curfew and went out to a restaurant. When they returned, their passports had been pointedly placed on their beds in empty rooms. 'Nothing was said,' Moore recalls, 'not until Saturday, when we were training in Estoril. We were going to play an eight-a-side and Alf said, "Out you go . . . except the seven." We stayed behind uncomfortably, and he said: "I don't admire what you've done and if I had enough members here to make up a team, none of you would play, you'd be on a plane. Make sure it doesn't happen again."' A new era, indeed.

England won the match 4-3, with Cohen now at right-back and Thompson, Liverpool's thrilling winger, on the opposite flank to Charlton; Eastham and Milne being the midfield pair in a 4-2-4 formation. Haynes was long gone, his international career ended following a car crash in Blackpool. It was with this formation that Ramsey took his team to Rio for what was termed a 'Little World Cup', in which they would lose to Brazil and Argentina, causing Ramsey to undertake a major re-think. With Pelé rampant and Gerson mastering the middle of the field, England suffered their biggest defeat since losing 5-0 to Yugoslavia in 1958. For the first hour England held their own, but Pelé was almost untouchable, beating four men to create the first goal. Yet even more impressive, tactically, were Argentina, who defeated Brazil in a robust final, watched by England. With fruit and vegetables flying through the air at half-time from an irate crowd in the Maracana Stadium, Ramsey got to his feet and said to his players with typical understatement: 'Well, gentlemen, I'm ready. Shall we go?' and proceeded to lead them out across one corner of the pitch. Cohen recalls: 'Argentina were playing 4-4-2 and it was one of the best displays I had yet seen. Rattin was outstanding, and we knew then they'd be a danger in the World Cup. There was a lot Alf learned from that visit.'

These set-backs renewed some of the doubts at home, unfairly, and although in the season 1964-65, England won six and drew four of their ten matches, the criticism mounted almost unbearably. The low point was reached with the 1-1 draw away to Holland in mid-winter, Greaves scoring the only goal. Afterwards, Ramsey was surrounded by a crowd of hostile journalists claiming that England had no chance for the World Cup on this form.

Doggedly, stone-faced and impassive, he stood his ground, arguing till late in the evening with one of the more belligerent journalists from Manchester. As in his first season, Ramsey was to re-establish his and the team's credibility with the summer tour, drawing with Yugoslavia, defeating West Germany and Sweden. It was in Belgrade that one of the definitive Ramsey-style players made his debut: Alan Ball, the mercurial little midfield player from Blackpool with red hair and a temperament to match.

The day before the match, Ramsey approached Ball during training. 'Are you all right young man?' 'Yes,' said Ball, bouncing about like a yo-yo. 'Well, stop kicking the ball around, I want to talk to you. Do you think you're ready to play for England?' 'Yes,' Ball said. 'Then you're playing tomorrow.' Ball was still nineteen, and would be twenty on the day they beat Germany in Nuremberg. He was dynamic, almost absurdly dedicated to the game, to the extent that as a teenager he did nothing to cure his adolescent spots in the hope that they would keep the girls away and allow him to devote himself exclusively to football. Ball, who moved into management, repays the conviction that Ramsey showed towards them: 'The fellow was complete – tactically aware, thorough, had his own idea how the game should be played, was approachable, could put you right. I never found a flaw in him, and I've played with a few managers: Suart, Catterick, Mee, Neill, McMenemy. That day in Belgrade, Alf told me not to worry how I played, just *play*. He promised I'd play enough times to find out if I could make it. He dispelled the idea with anyone that they only got one chance.'

For the past three matches the centre-half had been Jack Charlton, who had made his debut in the 2-2 draw with Scotland, together with Stiles. The Ramsey formula was taking shape. 'I once asked Alf, why me?' Jack told me. 'He said it was because I was tall and good in the air and was mobile and could tackle. He knew how he wanted to play, and went out to get the right type for him – not necessarily the best players, but the best for his plan. There was enormous pressure on him from the media, especially the London press. It's easy to see how a manager's mind can become inundated with names he may not have seen, but Alf's attitude was always "Don't tell me, I'll tell you." He had a *feel* for players. In a real team you can't have shit-stirrers around. If there's someone you don't trust, get rid of them. They were totally absent in that squad. I never once heard any player questioning the merits of another, whether he should or shouldn't be in. Alf was totally different from Don Revie, he achieved what he did with just a few words.'

Ramsey was a paradox. Having taken the trouble to adjust his speech to encompass a wider social span, he remained happiest among his own kind, tentative and often ill at ease when in public, hugely protective of his privacy to the point of suspicion. After England had drawn with Poland at Goodison Park in Liverpool, the night before the World Cup draw was made in London in January 1966, Ramsey was travelling the next morning to keep an appointment with a television company for whom he was to give comments on the draw. A television representative was there to meet him off the train at Euston. As Ramsey came down the platform, the man approached him. 'Excuse me, are you Alf Ramsey?' he enquired. 'What's that got to do with you?' demanded the ever defensive Alf.

He could deliver the driest of one-liners. When, six months later, England played the return friendly in Poland a few days before the start of the World Cup, Ramsey had reluctantly agreed to the switching of the match from Warsaw to Katovice, necessitating a grinding two-hour bus journey on bad roads. Half-way through what seemed an interminable trip, a rather nervous interpreter enquired of Ramsey what he would like to do later in the evening. 'To get to Katovice, I hope,' an unsmiling Ramsey replied. Having won the match, the squad were returning to their hotel and due to have a two-day break with their families on arriving home the next day. On the bus they all started singing: 'Good, Night, Alfie, we'll – see – you on Fri-day.' Whereupon Ramsey stood up and announced: 'Yes, at two o'clock sharp.'

Without surrendering his authority, he was able to enjoy a banter and camaraderie with the players which fostered their mutual respect. This was something which Winterbottom had either never allowed or been able to achieve. Playing in Madrid that winter – a milestone in the team's development which will be discussed later – Ramsey was taking part in an eight-a-side during training, when he was summarily up-ended in a tackle by Cohen, landing upside-down. Looking up from the ground with a pained expression, Ramsey mockingly rebuked him. 'If I had another effing full-back, you'd not be playing tomorrow.' George was another of his dependables, and could afford to laugh with him. Indeed, they all could. 'When I first started playing with England, there would be new faces nearly every time, and there were always cliques,' Wilson says, 'but with Alf, nobody had an edge, there was nobody you had to look up to. A team out of that squad could have won the First Division title, which you can't say about many international teams.'

Ramsey contrived to strike a rare balance between discipline and affection for his players. On a plane to Mexico in 1969, to prepare for the defence of the World Cup the following year, Allan Clarke was living it up a bit with a few of the players. Ramsey wandered down the aisle. 'Enjoying yourself, Allan?' he asked.

'Yes, great, thanks Alf,' Clarke replied. Reprovingly, Ramsey said: 'You don't enjoy yourself with me. Remember that.' Ramsey knew instinctively when to apply a brake on a particular player, yet was sensitive to the occasional need for a reassuring word. When Ball was somewhat unluckily sent off on one occasion, the knocking on his bedroom door late in the evening was the manager coming to commiserate and tell him not to be disheartened.

One of the most generous gestures I have ever witnessed in sport came after England's defeat in the 1970 quarter-final against West Germany. The luckless Bonetti of Chelsea, having taken over at the last moment from a suddenly sick Banks, had made profound errors which contributed to two if not three of Germany's goals as they recovered from two down. As the squad prepared afterwards for a dejected return to London, a genuine chance to retain the Cup away from home having been squandered, Ramsey was walking around the lawn of their hotel in Leon to thank the players for their efforts. He came to Bonetti. 'Thank you so much for all you have done, I hope you have a good journey home,' Ramsey said, with a sincerity which most men at that moment would have found impossible.

His career was dealt disasters as well as triumphs, and with all of them, as Kipling advocated, Ramsey remained level-headed. Bonetti would never play again for his country, but this was no moment for recrimination. It helped to make Alf the best manager any of his players had ever known.

4

A National Club

'IT WAS ABOUT relationships,' Jack Charlton says, reflecting upon the unity which Ramsey managed to establish in a squad that met only every month or so. 'The remarkable thing about the group, whether it was training at Lilleshall, meeting at Hendon Hall or on tour, was how well everyone got on together. It's never been there before or since Alf's day, and it's even rare to find it in a club squad. It didn't matter what you did – play cards, go for a walk – everyone joined in, you did it with whoever happened to be there at the moment. I love seeing all the others, we're all pals, still. I feel comfortable in their company.'

Ramsey may have formed, uniquely, a national club, but the 1965-66 season began poorly. A goalless draw with Wales in Cardiff was followed by England's third home defeat only by a foreign side when Austria won 3-2. Slack in defence and finishing poorly in attack, England allowed Austria twice to come from behind; and nine minutes from time Stiles was dispossessed twenty yards out by Fritsch, who shot the ball over Springett, stranded out near the penalty spot. The wrath of the critics once more pounded Ramsey's ears, the more loudly because, in his provocative way, he had stated after the match: 'I'm not very disappointed, just disappointed.' Prospects in the World Cup were rated slim by the public. For some, Ramsey had taken on the appearance of Captain Bligh, controversial leader adrift in an open boat. Yet part of Ramsey's private satisfaction against Austria was the performance of Bobby Charlton who, having missed England's summer tour, was now for the first time filling a midfield role to good effect. It was a key to the immediate future.

Part of the criticism for the failure against Austria was directed at Greaves, who had missed simple chances. It was not long after this that he was found to have hepatitis, a severe form of jaundice, which would put him out of the game for ten weeks, including three internationals and twelve league matches. He did not return with Spurs until mid-January. 'Brian Curtin, the club doctor, wasn't sure at first how bad it was, but when I got to the Royal Free Hospital, Sheila Sherlock, the consultant, thought it was unlikely I would play again that season,' Greaves recalls.

One of England's goals against Austria was scored by Connelly. In the next match, at home against Northern Ireland, on a damp November evening when Baker replaced Greaves, Thompson and Connelly appeared on what was to be the last occasion in the modern game when England would use two old-fashioned conventional wingers. When, twelve years later, Ron Greenwood used Coppell and Peter Barnes in a fluid 4-4-2, Coppell could be regarded as part midfield player, and the same was true of Chamberlain of Stoke when Bobby Robson briefly used him and John Barnes in the summer of 1984. Thompson and Connelly helped beat Ireland 2-1, the effervescent Baker having a fine match and scoring the first goal. Connelly, who was part of Burnley's classic team of that era, played half his twenty international matches with Winterbottom, half with Ramsey, scoring a useful seven goals. 'I enjoyed playing with Alf, and was able to continue playing with him as a normal winger,' Connelly says. 'It helped, of course, that I could go down flanks. It was a magic squad, and I was really involved right up to the start of the World Cup. Alf was always looking for *blend*, but by now he was settled with his back four, and Bobby Charlton and Stiles were also fixtures. That only left changes open in four positions up front. Yet there was no personal rivalry in the squad at all, which was very unusual. At the time when it had seemed that Nobby and Alan Ball might be competing for a place, you couldn't have found a pair more happy and humorous together. Mind you, I'd been brought up in a good club. Harry Potts, the manager, could be a right swine when he chose, but he had the deepest affection for us players.' (As an aside, Connelly had made his England debut in 1959 against Wales in a match which saw one of the two appearances Brian Clough made before injury put him out of the game.)

A month later, on a bitterly cold December night, England gained their first victory in Spain with a performance that was doubly innovative and a turning-point in Ramsey's career. He introduced for the first time a 4-3-3 formation, with Stiles, Bobby Charlton and Eastham in midfield, and Hunt replacing Thompson in an attack with Ball and Baker (which left no place for Connelly): and the shirt numbers on the players' backs suddenly had no relevance. The system was a revelation to many foreigners, let alone English observers, and combined ingenuity with simplicity. The vulnerability of two link men in a 4-2-4 formation – Haynes and Robson in Winterbottom's time, Eastham and Milne in the 'Little World Cup' eighteen months previously – had been overcome by an all-round flexibility.

'We can defend with eight and attack with eight,' observed Ramsey, implying that the full-backs as well as the midfield three were expected to compensate for the absence of wingers. To function satisfactorily, however, the system was dependent on a quality to loom ever larger in the game's language: work-rate. And where would Greaves fit into such a system, if and when he was fit again?

'Before Alf, we'd never had a plan away from home, and this new development was really something,' Bobby Charlton says. 'My change from wing to midfield had first happened at Old Trafford. When Alf made the switch to 4-3-3, he particularly made the point that we weren't going to become a defensive team, that the three up front wouldn't be alone, that we'd have six up front. He was defensive of his own plan, that it should not be seen as defensive. It was a system that enabled strangers, new players, to be brought in and to fit.'

The second goal in a 2-0 win in Madrid was scored by Hunt, who as much as anyone was to characterise the selflessness of the new system. He had made his debut as long ago as 1962 under Winterbottom, scoring together with Crawford and Flowers in the 3-1 home win against Austria, but thereafter had made only intermittent appearances as unofficial deputy for Greaves. 'It *was* a different system with England, none of us had played it at club level,' he reflects. Hunt had played only four times previously with Ramsey. 'I was fighting my way into the team at that time, but I felt, with the World Cup being in England and never losing many games at home, that we did have a chance, though it was difficult to judge, not being a regular member. Shanks [Bill Shankly] never made much comment about it at Anfield. He was a typical Scot, he didn't like England to do well. He respected Alf, but I think he wanted us to lose!' England's captain was more emphatic about the significance of that victory. 'There's always a benefit from winning away, but that was something new,' Moore says. 'Alf's changes were gradual, and that's the secret of selection: finding the right players and then using them in the positions in which you'll get the most out of them. And the only way you get cameraderie to develop is to allow time. It's the "time-after-match" factor, when you're doing things together, that creates it. A good team on the field is a good team off the field.'

An irony of England's togetherness was in fact the temperamental distance between the Charlton brothers. Bobby recalls the day they were youngsters and playing in separate matches on adjacent pitches and Jack gave away a penalty. Walking home, the twelve-year-old Bobby pulled his brother's leg, saying, 'Fancy doing a thing like that.' 'Jack didn't say a word. He just thumped me.' Years later, they were playing against each other in the 1965 FA Cup semi-final at Nottingham when Jack heard on the radio that he'd been given his first cap against Scotland. Bobby had not heard the broadcast and, wondering whether he himself was included, asked his brother if he was in. 'I dunno,' Jack said. They much respect each other, but are quite independent.

After the euphoria of the Madrid victory England came down to earth, or more accurately, mud, just over a month later when they played Poland at Goodison the night before the World Cup draw. On a glue-pot pitch, Poland took the lead just before half-time and England only equalised with a quarter of an hour to go. Gordon Harris of Burnley, deputising for the injured Bobby Charlton, won the ball in midfield and pushed it out to Cohen on the right. Going past two opponents, Cohen ended his run with one of his more accurate crosses and Bobby Moore, having advanced to the far post, headed home for one of his two goals in 108 matches. 'I think that was just about my best game for England,' Cohen says. 'I had a pat on the back afterwards from Paul Reaney, of Leeds, which was very generous, because Paul was pushing me hard for a place. Frankly, if Ramsey had not been manager, I don't think I'd have got a smell. I was never comfortable with Winterbottom when I played eight times for the Under 23 team. I wasn't a natural footballer. I had to work a lot at things, but I knew my asset was my strength and speed, which I developed to a point where I was almost an even-time sprinter. Although I used to get forward a lot, Ramsey emphasised that I was first a defender. That was my forte, I'd had a good grounding at Fulham, my only club. I could tackle, and read the game reasonably well. Alf only asked you to do what you were capable of doing. By this time, I'd got a good relationship with Gordon [Banks]. I'd go for everything unless he said leave it. There were two men you could count on, Gordon and Jack; there was little we lost in the air. When Bobby scored his goal, I remember he went straight back to the half-way line. No fuss. That was him. I was very lucky, all the managers I played with were good. Dugald Livingstone at Fulham had been a full-back himself, and made me one instead of wing-half. Then there was Bedford Jezzard, a nice man, and Vic Buckingham. Vic was very blasé, but he taught me a lot. He'd been with Ajax and Barcelona, and I never trained or worked harder with anyone. He was ahead of his time.'

It was another cross by Cohen which led to the only goal against West Germany at Wembley, when England fielded only five of the side which would appear there six months later with rather more at stake. Cohen's cross was headed through Tilkowski's hands by Hunt and forced over the line by Stiles – his only international goal. The significance of this match was the first appearance of the former young wing-half from West Ham, now converted to centre-forward: Geoff Hurst. He had originally been switched there by Greenwood to create a partner for Johnny Byrne, himself an England candidate but a totally different style of player, a marvellously dexterous ball-player. Byrne, one of the most gifted I have seen but pre-disposed to self-indulgence both on the ball and at the bar, had been denied a place in the squad in Chile only by the prejudice of a selector from West Bromwich, against whom Byrne had deliberately conceded a penalty by fisting the ball over the bar, West Brom missing the kick! Of Hurst, it was said by a national columnist: 'It's not Ramsey's fault if there is not a decent centre-forward in the country. Hurst isn't an orthodox leader, but could be the next best thing.'

Hurst kept his place: and scored in the 4-3 victory over Scotland at Hampden, something even better for morale than winning in Madrid. Hunt (2) and Bobby Charlton scored the other goals in front of a crowd of 134,000. It was England's first win over the old enemy since 1961, and the first for Ramsey, the more rewarding because Scotland at that time had some formidable players: Murdoch, Bremner and Baxter in midfield; Johnstone of Celtic, Law, Wallace and Johnston of Rangers in attack in a 3-3-4 formation. The wee Johnstone, bewilderingly clever, took an unfortunate Newton, deputising for Wilson, for a lively dance and scored twice. For England, Ball was now operating from midfield and Connelly had come back on the left flank. Bobby Charlton put England 4-2 in front with a blistering shot from twenty-five yards.

Much of Scotland's sting was absorbed by Stiles, a year after his debut against them in London. He had got his chance then, strangely enough, when Mullery, who had been expected to play, ricked his neck while shaving. At Old Trafford, Stiles had earned the nickname of 'Happy', donated by Chay Brennan, on account of the fact that in training and during matches Stiles could usually be found chastising one of his colleagues. He was a galvanic leader. When playing for England schoolboys he had been described by the *Sunday Times* as a 'player in the mould of Coluna of Portugal'. As an attacking wing-half for his school, St Patrick's of Collyhurst, he had the most goals in a season, but his role for Ramsey was different. 'When I went to Old Trafford in 1957, there were Edwards, Colman and Charlton in the *reserves'* dressing room – and United still wanted me!' he recalls. 'They were great days. We used to go to West Brom' – where in 1985 he was trying to save the club from decline, as manager, and win or lose by the odd goal in seven. Often I'd be on at Bobby to hold it. He was a great competitor, worked so hard and cared so much. But he loved to hit those long balls, and if I had a go at him, he felt it an insult. I was a great moaner.'

But it was the Scots who were moaning this time. 'We stuffed them, and we loved it,' Connelly says. 'If they beat you, you had it pushed at you all week by the Scots back at your club and right up till you played them again next year.' With Stiles unfit, there was an important and possibly fortuitous change for the last home match before the World Cup, against Yugoslavia. Martin Peters made his debut in a team with six changes. Cohen was also injured, Armfield returning for the first time for two years: as captain, because Hunter replaced Moore. Tambling of Chelsea, whose only previous full cap had been won three years earlier, replaced Connelly, while Greaves, now recovered from hepatitis, displaced Hunt. After only nine minutes Greaves, with a rare header, scored the first of England's two goals from a cross by Paine – replacement for Ball – and inevitably the headlines next morning proclaimed: 'Greaves Comes Back', never mind that Bobby Charlton's second goal was the more spectacular.

Ramsey had bristled in defence of those who had been left out. 'Moore has not been dropped, none of them has,' he had insisted. 'Since I took over, I have said over and over again that I have never had a team but a squad. It's no use having a first team and a number of reserves. They have all got to be ready to step into the team. I have picked a team against Yugoslavia to see what certain players and combinations can achieve. This is the last match before selecting the twenty-two for the World Cup and going on tour. It is fair to assume that a number of players are on trial. Too often in the past we have been dependent on players who become injured or lose form. It is likely to happen to one or two in the World Cup squad before the start, so I must know exactly who can do what.'

It had been an anxious match for Greaves, aware that the team had been acquiring a new shape in his absence. 'I knew I had to push myself hard to get back. I was one of the few who believed we'd win [the World Cup] and also that I would be part, so the race was on to get fit. I did, but not one hundred per cent, I think, though I'm not sure I ever was! But people did say I'd lost my edge.'

For Peters, it had been something of an unexpected summons. Three years earlier he had been a third choice selection for an Under 23 match with Winterbottom, scored a couple of goals from outside the penalty area, played in another three or four, and made his only appearance for Ramsey in an Under 23 match against Wales at Bristol in 1964. 'Then, nothing until 1966,' Peters says, subsequently having worked for a motor insurance company alongside Hurst, following their various managerial efforts with different clubs after retirement as players. 'Until three months before the Yugoslavia match I hadn't even been mentioned in despatches. Then I had an Under 23 match at Blackburn against Turkey, didn't score, and it came down the grapevine that Alf thought I couldn't head the ball. I'd had a varying three seasons – lost my place at West Ham in '63, when they went on to win the cup, got back the next season at centre-half, moved to left-back, then to right-half when Eddie Bovingdon was injured, and was then never out. Being selected against Yugoslavia was joining the elite, although I hadn't taken much notice of the national team, being more concerned with my club place, and playing for Ramsey didn't really enter my head until Geoff got in against Germany. Admittedly, I was in the preliminary forty for the World Cup, and apparently Greenwood was pushing Ramsey for me to have a go. Not that there was too much difference in the way England played, I found. West Ham aligns you for international football, though that's why it's probably difficult for them to win the league. That first game, I tended to let Bobby [Charlton] and Jimmy have the ball, but later I started more to do what was instinctive.'

Moore at this time was in dispute with West Ham and the day after the Yugoslavia match Billy Wright, the Arsenal manager, made a transfer bid for him. The following week Pickering, the Everton centre-forward who earlier had made three appearances for Ramsey, was dropped by Harry Catterick on the eve of the Cup Final and Trebilcock, his deputy, scored twice as Everton came from two down to beat Sheffield Wednesday. Alex Stepney became the world's most expensive goalkeeper when transferred from Millwall to Chelsea for £40,000 . . . and on 14 June, Wright was sacked at the end of four years in charge at Highbury.

England were now gathered for an eleven-day period of intensive training, in what some of them regarded as the monastic isolation of the Lilleshall national recreation centre in rural Shropshire. This time, however, there was not the antipathy or moody displeasure which had existed four years earlier at Coya. Some, indeed, enjoyed the pastoral tranquillity. 'It's beautiful, isn't it, the sort of place you go miles to see,' Flowers said on the first day. Stiles was more pragmatic. 'Well, we wouldn't all choose it, but it's got to be done, hasn't it, and that's all there is to it. Certainly, they don't have grass like this in Manchester.' Greaves, as ever, had slightly the air of a *bon viveur* reduced to diet pills. Big Jack was typically blunt, and called it a prison, but says he doesn't recall hearing a word of complaint from the others.

There was a strict schedule from 9.00 a.m. to 9.00 p.m.: after breakfast, training through the morning; games of various sorts in the afternoon, tea, a bath, dinner, films, and bed. There was the ritual daily award of a yellow jersey to the player who had least distinguished himself during the afternoon's sports. Moore, still at odds with West Ham, and said by the press to be under threat from Hunter for his place, was in a pensive mood: merely one of a crowd. Peters telephoned Kathy, his wife, to say he thought he had no chance of making the final twenty-two.

There was a medical every day with Alan Bass, the doctor, and weights were checked. 'We've got athletes' foot down to thirty per cent of what it was when the players came together,' Bass said at the conclusion of the camp. 'And we've got them cutting their toe-nails properly. There were only five out of the twenty-seven who knew how. It's incredible. You wouldn't find that sort of thing with ballet dancers, yet these fellows get far more money than all but the top dancers.'

Jack was more worried about getting out for a quiet pint than about his toe-nails. 'It was like being in a Stalag, standing by the gate at the end of the drive and watching people walking by. By the end of the first week it was a dream, to get out and go to the pub, but the boat was only rocked once. A couple of the lads went to the golf course, and managed to get a couple of shandies there. There was hell to pay when Alf found out, but he hadn't said we couldn't go.'

'The one anxiety was to get into the final twenty-two,' Ball says. 'We all worked so hard. I was *so* fit. The training was *so* competitive. The cameraderie was great even though five of us were going to go out.' On the morning of 18 June, as the squad made its way back from the training pitch, past the landscaped shrubbery and the formal flower beds, Ramsey one by one called aside the five. Hurst remembers it as the longest walk of his life, staring ahead and hoping not to hear his name. The five who did were Johnny Byrne of West Ham, Gordon Milne of Liverpool, Keith Newton of Blackburn, Bobby Tambling of Chelsea and Peter Thompson of Liverpool. The squad, announced with the traditional positioning, would be:

GOALKEEPERS: Gordon Banks (Leicester), Ron Springett (Sheffield Wednesday), Peter Bonetti (Chelsea).
FULL-BACKS: Jimmy Armfield (Blackpool), Ray Wilson (Everton), George Cohen (Fulham), Gerry Byrne (Liverpool).
HALF-BACKS: Nobby Stiles (Manchester United), Martin Peters (West Ham), Jack Charlton (Leeds), Ron Flowers (Wolverhampton Wanderers), Bobby Moore (West Ham), Norman Hunter (Leeds).

36

FORWARDS: Terry Paine (Southampton), Ian Callaghan (Liverpool), Jimmy Greaves (Tottenham Hotspur), Roger Hunt (Liverpool), Geoff Hurst (West Ham), Bobby Charlton (Manchester United), Alan Ball (Blackpool), George Eastham (Arsenal), John Connelly (Manchester United).

'I was most surprised that I got in and Peter [Thompson] didn't,' Ian Callaghan says. It *was* surprising, for he was a young member of the Liverpool side who had yet to make his international debut, whereas Thompson was an established figure. It was a further guide to Ramsey's mood, which provoked a new wave of public excitement, when in the first of the four matches on tour against Finland he omitted Moore and Greaves and included Callaghan. Finland were beaten 3-0 and speculation about Moore was rife. Yet those who doubted his ability, or the manager's ultimate confidence in him, proved to be way off the mark. There was not much doubt within the squad. 'I always took him for granted,' Bobby Charlton says. 'I never thought anyone should play instead of him. He had such vision that he rarely had to make a last ditch tackle.' Cohen's view is that the team was so mature the captaincy hardly mattered. 'Players recognised Bobby as outstanding, yet I was club captain, Jack was the senior pro at Leeds, Hunt was a pillar at Liverpool, Wilson was the best left-back in the world apart from Facchetti of Italy, Ball was a law unto himself. Who needed captaining?' Wilson recognises the gulf there was between some of Moore's performances for club and country. 'Maybe he was complacent,' he says. 'He had this capacity to alter with circumstances. If it was the World v. Mars, Bobby would be on top. He wasn't the same player for West Ham.'

Moore himself admits that Ramsey caused him a missed heartbeat. 'Everyone in the squad was aware different players would get an opportunity, because Alf had said he'd be trying to play everyone if he could during the tour,' Moore says. 'Yet it was a warning, and I thought "Oh! Right." Alf didn't speak much about the captaincy, though he had asked me before I took over from Jimmy Armfield in 1963 whether I wanted the job, was I aware of the responsibility? It was a vote of confidence and support as much as anything [as a player] when he appointed me. I did not really influence him as captain, it was such a good era, we knew numerous players could have come in, because the backbone was established. He'd have a quiet word with me about what he intended, to keep me informed, but only after he had made up his mind. He never consulted me on [selecting] a player. When he left me out in Finland, he never said anything! Norman was playing well, Leeds were successful, and I was in disagreement with West Ham. People may have thought my mind was on other things. It may have been his way of saying, "I know what's going on, show me you want it." It did create a doubt, showed me I'd got to work at it.'

For the following match in Oslo, Moore returned in one of nine changes. Hurst was left out. Hunt was paired with Greaves, and the little man celebrated the occasion by scoring four, to carry him past Bobby Charlton as England's leading goal-scorer at that stage. Though scoring first, Norway offered little resistance, England taking charge with three in three minutes by Greaves (2) and Connelly. Stiles trotted off at the finish observing wryly, 'That wasn't bad for the second team.' Greaves dismisses suggestions that it was nothing more than a doddle. 'You've still got to put the ball in the net, haven't you? And we've seen a few weak teams since then playing England without the goals being scored. I felt after Oslo that I'd cracked it, and when we beat Poland at the end of the tour I was sure that Roger and I would be the front two.'

Two days later, in Copenhagen, Joe Mears, the mild-mannered chairman of the FA and of Chelsea Football Club, was suddenly taken ill, and died: a kindly man, who had played in goal for the Old Malvernians and was now sadly denied, by no more than a month on the one hand and less than a year on the other, the joy of seeing fulfilled his ambition for England to win the World Cup and Chelsea to reach a post-war FA Cup Final. Against Denmark, Hurst was re-introduced and, though England won by two goals, considered it was 'the worst performance of my international career'. Denmark held out until a minute before half-time, and an otherwise friendly game was marred by some reckless tackling by Jack Charlton and Stiles, who left behind no friends and provided an ill omen for the weeks to come. The success of the match was Ball, who attributed his performance to his growing maturity and a degree of control over his temper. After discussion between Ramsey, Dr Bass and Harold Shepherdson, the trainer and physiotherapist, the players were allowed a free evening for the first time in three weeks: they would not have another for the next month.

From Copenhagen, the party then made the laborious trip to Katovice, via Warsaw. Ramsey selected what he regarded at this stage as his strongest team: no Hurst. In front of the shrilly whistling crowd of 75,000, in the dank grey surroundings of Chorzow Stadium, Hunt scored the only goal in the thirteenth minute. Put through by Bobby Charlton on the left, Hunt dummied to pass to Greaves outside him, turned inside and hit a wonderful shot from thirty yards – probably the best of his eighteen goals for England in thirty-four matches.

It was the second time that Ball and Peters had played together. Peters, omitted against Norway and Denmark, had thought himself again left out when Ramsey, announcing the team to the players, named Stiles at No. 4, which was the shirt Peters had worn on his first two appearances. Now he was caught by surprise, when out came his name in the final position at No. 11. Although Peters had played in every single position for West Ham, even he was not yet fully accustomed to the fact that the number on his back no longer always signified his position. The selection in Poland meant that for the first time Ramsey was using a 4-4-2 formation, with Greaves and Hunt alone up front: thereby inevitably increasing the problems, physical and temperamental, for Greaves. Ramsey, however, was understandably happy. He said after the match: 'This is the toughest team we have met on the tour, and this [planning] was quite deliberate. We wanted to build up gradually and it has worked out well, but I still cannot be satisfied. I am sure that some day some side is going to get a hell of a licking from England.'

The manager's confidence, and that of his squad, was high; the more so as he had told them after watching Brazil draw 2-2 in Sweden that 'Brazil are no danger, they're too old.' His judgement was not often adrift. He had said England would win the Cup and now, with six days to go to the start, most of his men believed him. 'The tour made me realise we could do it,' Wilson says. 'We'd moved into a different league.'

5

England Stutter: Brazil Speechless

11 JULY　　　　　　　　**B**EFORE THE DRAW had been made in January, the Uruguayan Ambassador in London had suggested to Sir Stanley Rous, the President of FIFA, that the opening match should be between England, the hosts, and his own country, first ever winners of the Cup. When this was decreed by the draw, the Ambassador was convinced that Rous must have 'fixed' it – it is not new for people to suppose that the draw is less than fair and square – and when the Queen arrived at Wembley, she found waiting for her a massive gift from the Uruguayan in the form of a bullock wagon worked in copper, and mounted on a trolley. It proved to be the last moment of South American generosity in that competition. Rous himself had been busy trying to ensure fair play off the pitch, establishing facilities for dope testing, with two players from each team to be tested after every match. 'We wanted to make sure that there should be no accusations of teams receiving shots in the arm,' he recalled.

To the stirring sight of the massed bands of the guards, providing a moving sea of colour, and the sounds of Empire echoing round the Mecca of football, a crowd of only 75,000 poured early into the stadium. Young boys carrying placards for the sixteen finalists led a parade which, by the extravagant standards that have now become commonplace, was indeed a modest opening ceremony. When the Queen shook hands with the teams before the match she observed to Moore, as he introduced her to the England players, that the red, white and blue of the floral display were the right colours. 'I hope they bring you luck,' she said with a smile.

It was only a few days previously that Moore had cleared himself to be eligible to play, by signing a one-month contract with West Ham to qualify as a registered player, as required by FIFA regulations. Enthusiasm was at fever pitch across the country as Istvan Zsolt, the Hungarian referee, looked at his watch to blow the first whistle of the Cup: the fact that some 25,000 seats were not filled was partly a consequence of live television, which resulted in touts being left standing outside with fistfuls unsold, but also because many people had taken fright at the likely traffic jams.

Matt Busby had seen Uruguay playing in a preparatory match in Lisbon, and had returned home with the opinion that 'they don't have one redeeming feature'. The entire football world was about to endorse this view. The Uruguayans were living on past glories and present fears. They had won the Olympic tournaments of 1924 and 1928, the World Cups of 1930 and 1950. 'As other people think of their patriotic history, we think of our football,' Ondino Viera, their manager, had said beforehand. Now, they thought only of survival: immediately the first ball was kicked, more than half their team fled back into defence, where they would remain for the next ninety minutes. It was an undignified capitulation by Juan Lopez, their coach and the man who had been in charge when they had defeated Brazil at Maracana, Rio, to win the Cup sixteen years before. England had fifteen corners and sixteen shots at goal, but could never find a way through a blanket of eight or nine defenders.

Ramsey's only change from the team which had given such optimism in Poland was to re-introduce Connelly in place of Peters. It was to be a particularly frustrating match for this amiable and willing winger on what would prove to be his last international appearance. Sitting relaxed in his little restaurant in the old Lancashire mill country, with a painting of the Burnley– Spurs Cup Final on the wall behind him, his laughing brown eyes unoffended as he recollected how his career had taken a wrong turn, he said: 'We really gave their full-backs stick in that match, but somehow we weren't getting over the crosses. I was surprised, and glad, to be back in the team because I knew Alf had an admiration for Peters, who was a very good player. I'd played fairly well in my matches against Scotland, Norway and Denmark – you *know* when you're going well. But Uruguay was a bad one to come back for. They were determined they weren't going to lose. I hit the bar and scraped the post. I was told later I got a bit of criticism on television, that the commentators had some laughs. It's all right for them, they stay on. The crowd had applause for Bobby Moore, playing at the back with Jack, and I remember thinking, "He should try it up here." Up front, we were three against eight some of the time. I couldn't believe it: in the next match against Mexico, there were so many people going forward. If we'd scored against Uruguay, maybe the team would have stayed the same.'

Wilson recollects that he spent much of the match standing watching on the half-way line. 'They had ten full-backs and a goalkeeper. No team would have done well against them, we felt we'd played as well as we were allowed to.' Uruguay made barely a couple of chances. Banks once had to save when Cortes, their midfield player, let fly from twenty-five yards, and in the second half Rocha, turning tightly past Jack Charlton a yard outside the penalty area, hit a cross shot which beat Banks and went wide. Greaves, Hunt and Connelly were constantly smothered, Hunt's heavy-footed persistence insufficient against such defensive tactics. 'We lasted better than they did,' Greaves says, 'and should have scored in the last twenty minutes. Yet if we were still playing them today we probably wouldn't have scored.'

Ball, operating in midfield, was contemptuously dismissed by one commentator, who would be praising him to the skies a fortnight later, as someone 'who will never be a winger if he lives to be a hundred'. That was not Ramsey's intention, but for the moment his planning had misfired. Afterwards, he would only say that he was disappointed with the result but not the performance, and that he had known Uruguay were going to be tough. World Cup matches usually are: the bookmakers' odds on England immediately drifted from 3/1 to 4/1, with Brazil still favourites at 2 /1. Jack Charlton, Connelly, Hunt and Greaves left the scene of frustration so swiftly at the final whistle, while Uruguay danced and embraced in a mood of hollow triumph, that they missed the national anthem. Ramsey, ever pragmatic, told his men back in the dressing-room: 'You may not have won, but you didn't lose.' Never one to retreat, he was content to march slowly, even if his public and critics were not. 'This was a bad English team,' announced the report in *La Stampa* by Vittorio Pozzo, veteran manager of Italy's winning teams of 1934 and 1938. Hans Korfer was even more emphatic for *Sports Informations Dienst*. 'England will *not* win the World Cup.' Hunt was openly more truthful than his manager. 'It was a big let-down for everyone. We were short on ideas. Like all South Americans they looked good on the ball.' They also now had as good a chance as England of reaching the quarter-final from Group I.

12 JULY. In Group II in the Midlands, Helmut Schoen was at this early stage less sure about the structure of his team than was Ramsey. He supposed it would be difficult to reach the last four in a group with Argentina, Spain and Switzerland, and was fortunate to be able to begin with comparatively easy opposition. Against Switzerland, at Hillsborough, West Germany scored five

without reply. Schoen dropped Emmerich, who had been so dangerous for Borussia Dortmund against Liverpool, preferring Brulls. Beckenbauer, who had made his debut as a nineteen-year-old the year before in a qualifying match against Sweden, and Haller, an emigre with Bologna, scored two each. The Swiss had no answer to the tireless industry of Seeler and the subtle yet tenacious Overath. 'I had some concern about Overath,' Schoen says. 'He was a great player, yet found it hard to discipline his temper because he was a battler, like Billy Bremner, and I hoped beforehand that the referees would let him into the game. He was too often speaking to the referee, much like Ball.'

Brazil, surrounded by an aura of invincibility after winning the Cup twice in succession, had been the focal point of interest beforehand in Group III in the north west: however much doubt there might be among saner judges about the decision by Vicente Feola, their ageing manager, to retain his old guard defenders, Djalmar Santos, Bellini and Orlando, who had almost a century of years between them. Garrincha, following an operation and a turbulent family life, was no longer the player he had been. But, of course, there was always Pelé, the genius of a thousand senior matches in ten years, though still no more than twenty-five. 'The only rest I get is when I'm injured,' he had lamented at Brazil's leafy headquarters at Lymm, where an indulgent hotel proprietor fussed over his famous guests as though they were his godchildren.

There were plenty of opponents who were only too intent to ensure that Pelé should quickly get some rest, the first of them being Zhechev of Bulgaria in the opening match at Goodison, where a crowd of 48,000 Merseysiders came to feast their eyes on the legendary South Americans. The fanatical followers of the Everton and Liverpool clubs would show themselves to be the most knowledgeable and appreciative of the competition. With Gerson nursing an ankle injury, Feola sent out a midfield pair of Denilson and Lima, and Brazil quickly had the upper hand. But Tschenscher, the West German referee, was soon at full stretch, attempting to cope with a profusion of fouls, many of them bestowed by Bulgaria upon Pelé. After one such by Yakimov after a quarter of an hour, Pelé himself shaped to take the kick from twenty yards. A line of four defenders formed a wall, and around it Pelé swerved a ferocious shot to which Naidenov could only get a couple of fingers as it ripped into the net.

After half an hour there was a mêlée of disorder in the centre circle as Pelé, his patience fraying, retaliated with a bad foul on Zhechev. Brazil's defence at times creaked against the fluid dribbling of Asparoukhov, a tall, imperious centre-forward who moved, like Albert of Hungary, with a balletic grace. He should have equalised when Gylmar, Brazil's normally sound goal-keeper, fumbled a back pass, but Asparoukhov ran the ball wide. Garrincha, with a marvellously struck away-swinging free kick, made Bulgaria pay the full price of their attempted intimidation with a second goal after half-time. The prize for Brazil was an injury which would keep Pelé out of their second match against Hungary.

There was a mystique about the North Koreans, with their strange-sounding oriental names, their two years' intensive training behind the communication curtain of Pyong Yang, and their nine goals in two qualifying play-off matches against Australia. The bubble burst at Middlesbrough. Fast, determined, but tiny, they were overpowered by the jack-booted Soviet Union, who were as methodical and unimaginative as ever. Khurtsilava, at the centre of their defence, gave a taste of physical excess yet to come as they put three goals past their communist colleagues. The surprise in the Soviet team was the absence of their captain Voronin. The following day Leonid Nikonov, their deputy minister of sport, gave the definitive Soviet sports press conference.

'How is it possible for you to drop your captain?'

'Ah, you are wrong. He is no longer captain, as he has not been selected.'

'But he is one of your best players.'

'No, at this time he is not.'

'Is he off form?'

'Voronin has to realise that a good player must train ever harder to reach higher peaks.'

'Can he do that within the next three days before you play Italy?'

'*We* will decide.'

13 JULY. Any expectation that France would emerge as serious rivals to England and Uruguay was dashed by the liveliness of a Mexican team temporarily escaping from their predictable limitations. Holding the French level at half-time, they scored four minutes afterwards. Padilla centred, Borja shot, Aubour in goal feebly failed to hold the ball low to his right, and Borja was able to follow up and score with a simple second attempt. Herbin, twenty years later to become the national manager, roused his colleagues and Hausser equalised with a drive which went in off a post. Borja squandered subsequent chances to give Mexico a victory, and an Israeli referee, Ashkenasi, increased the doubts that were growing about the control of the tournament on the field.

At Villa Park, Argentina quickly revealed the breadth of their skills when defeating Spain 2-1. Such renowned European players as Zoco, Del Sol, Suarez and Gento were over-shadowed by the wiles of Rattin, in midfield, and Onega and Mas in attack. Argentina had been denied the use of Sivori and Maschio, who had become naturalised in Europe. The temperature of the tackling, clearly encouraged by Juan Carlos Lorenzo, the Argentinian manager who had been appointed only two months before the finals, following the resignation in quick succession of two predecessors, bordered on the alarming. Roumentchev, the Bulgarian referee, appeared not to notice. Artimé's two goals for the winners might have been four had he taken all his chances.

Hungary's lack of a reliable goalkeeper was quickly to pull the rug from under perhaps the most exciting team in the competition. In the opening minute against Portugal at Old Trafford, Eusebio forced a corner. As the kick came over, Szentmihalyi was deceived by a feint by Torres, and Augusto was able to have an unopposed header from close range. Now a superb match developed for the ceaseless entertainment of a 30,000 crowd. Nagy gained control of the midfield duel with Coluna to drive Hungary forward, and repeatedly Farkas and Albert had the suspect Portuguese defence in difficulty. Bené, their right-winger, levelled the score and now it seemed that Hungary would accelerate clear. But a second demoralising error by Szentmihalyi, which had his colleagye Matrai beating the ground with his fists in dismay, critically turned the game. A centre by Torres bounced off the goalkeeper's chest, and Augusto was on hand to accept the offer. Portugal indulged in some adroit time-wasting and Torres headed a third from Eusebio's swerving corner as Hungarian morale foundered.

Sunderland had braced itself for a repeat of the indignities of the battle of Santiago four years earlier, in which Chile and Italy had needed to be separated by the police. The command of Italy, who scored through Mazzola within ten minutes, took the bones out of Chilean resistance. Technically clever as always, Rivera in a class of his own in midfield, Italy should have coasted, but could score no more than a second by Barison and exhibited a tameness of spirit which would eventually be their undoing.

15 JULY. French hearts raced when, on a wet and slippery pitch at the White City, 'Les Bleus' took the lead after a quarter of an hour against Uruguay. Simon was at this stage dominating the middle of the field, yet the goal was a result of Uruguayan panic – or cynicism – when Manicera grabbed Herbet round the waist and the Czech referee, Galba, encouragingly had no hesitation in awarding the penalty from which de Bourgoing scored. However, this provoked Uruguay to open their play for the first time yet,

beating their rivals at close quarters with disdainful ease, so that the early and exciting zest of the French forwards, Gondet especially, began to wane. Rocha equalised with a scrambled goal, then Cortes put them in front; doubts about Aubour were again raised when he missed the centre from the left. France pressed in the second half, but that only provided further openings for Uruguay which came and went thanks to profligate finishing by Sacia, who had been brought into the attack in place of Silva.

This narrow win put Uruguay temporarily in the strongest position in Group I, but up at Hillsborough, Spain kept Group II open when they disposed of Switzerland after being behind by a goal by Quentin at half-time. Ten minutes afterwards, Spain's right-back Sanchis scored a remarkable goal. Winning a tackle on the half-way line, he went off at speed, survived tackle after tackle and finally lashed the ball into the roof of the net. Suarez and Del Sol now took control of the game, but Spain were lucky when the Russian referee disallowed a second goal by Quentin for a foul on the goalkeeper. Back at the other end Suarez hit the bar from a free kick, and the winner came as Amaro took off headlong to meet a centre from Gento.

The frailties within the Brazilian camp, which bravado and a victory over Bulgaria had not disguised, now became fully apparent at Goodison Park, where Hungary produced a blistering exposition of uninhibited attack. Pelé was still injured and replaced by Tostao. For Djalmar Sanos, now thirty-seven, it was an echo of that famous confrontation in Berne eight years earlier, and once more Hungary were the victors on a rain-swept night that sent a crowd of 51,000 home in rapture. Despondent after their defeat by Portugal, Hungary had been buoyed by assurances from the old master, Puskas, in the intervening days, and by the optimism of Baroti, their manager, who knew their true worth. Hungary's four-man attack of Bené, Rakosi, Albert and Farkas took off like a pack of hounds and within three minutes had scored. Bené on the right beat Altair twice, continued with his swaying dribble past Bellini, and finally cut in to beat Gilmar on the near post, having first drawn him from his line.

The replacement of Szentmihalyi with Gelei in the Hungarian goal had done little to erase Hungary's vulnerability between the posts, which was soon confirmed when Gelei dropped a simple ball, though he was not at fault after a quarter of an hour when Tostao swept the ball in from a deflected free-kick from Lima. But with Gerson and Lima outwitted in the middle of the field and Albert untameable in attack, Brazil were done for. Garrincha was sadly seen to be a spent force, quite unable to inspire his colleagues in the absence of Pele. After an hour, Albert and Bené carved Brazil's left flank apart, and Farkas came through to meet

Bené's cross with a right-footed volley taken six inches off the ground for one of the most memorable goals of the finals. With Matrai injured for the last half-hour and Meszoly, who scored the third from a penalty, carrying his arm in a sling for the last fifteen minutes, Hungary triumphantly held on to inflict Brazil's first defeat since that meeting in Berne. At the finish, with the crowd chanting his name repeatedly, Albert stood in front of the main stand savouring the achievement as he drank from a bottle of water. 'At certain stages I felt they could equal the old team,' Baroti said, 'but with an average age of twenty-four they are almost four years younger. I felt before the start of the competition that we could do great things, and now perhaps we may.' The crowd had chanted, 'We want more' – as well they might; this had been real football.

Two minutes from the end at Middlesbrough, Pak Seung Zin caused delirium among North Koreans on and off the pitch when he upset Group IV calculations by equalising an earlier goal for Chile by Marcos. The Koreans were still alive.

16 JULY. The story of England against Mexico at Wembley was of the goal that transformed the host team, the catalyst of later confidence.

'I picked the ball up quite deep, and I had no intention of shooting at goal. I thought, well, I'll just carry it into their area and see what develops, you know, you might get someone that doesn't mark or someone that loses their position, and I didn't really expect them to allow me to keep going. Had someone come at me and challenged me, I would have laid it off to Geoff Hurst or Roger Hunt, or to Martin Peters or Alan Ball, but I just kept going, and all I could remember was seeing Roger going like that, diving in different directions and their defenders being pulled, and all of the time I was allowed to go further and further, and I carried to the left and I thought I'd just shift position and have another look, and I brought it to the right, and I thought I'm over the half-way line and I thought . . . it's lovely, Wembley, for shooting, you know, because the ball runs so smooth, it's very difficult to get the ball high off the floor and if you really whack it you've got a fair chance . . . and I thought if they let me go another half a dozen yards I'm going to have a dip, you know, and I brought it to the left-hand side and Roger went off and took a defender and it just opened up, and I remember a full-back, if I'm not mistaken, and I thought if *he* comes now I've had it, but he didn't, he stayed, and I just knocked it to the right and I thought, well, I've always been taught just hit it in the general direction of the goal and let the goalkeeper worry about it, and I just banged it and it came off so sweetly and when it was on its way I thought, well *that's* a goal, 'cos it was right up in the top, and I was very pleased with that.'

So was the nation. So was the 85,000 crowd at Wembley that Saturday night, as Bobby Charlton scored the most critical of his record forty-nine goals for England. For half an hour, England had been as frustrated as against Uruguay, quite unable to penetrate the ant-like cluster of plum red shirts across the Mexican penalty box, the Mexicans emerging out of the area like the start of a cross country race every time they won possession of the ball. It was a nonsense that such a team should be included in the finals at the expense of such nations as Sweden, Czechoslovakia and Scotland. Until Charlton broke the deadlock, the replacement of Ball and Connelly by Paine and Peters had effected no substantial improvement. Paine had been dazed by a blow in the first minute, and Hunt and Greaves had made little headway. In the second half England still lacked penetration until, fifteen minutes from the end, Bobby Charlton broke through on the left and slipped the ball to Greaves, whose shot was beaten out for Hunt to score. It was only England's fourth victory ever in the finals. Had they scored the four or five goals they should have had, it would have given them the option when playing France of going for a draw, so as to meet West Germany in the quarter-final rather than Argentina; though it must be doubtful if Ramsey would have flirted with such risk.

West Germany and Argentina had already drawn that afternoon without goals at Villa Park, so it would not be known who was the group winner until after their respective third matches. This had been a harsh affair, with Argentina revealing the more vicious side of their tactics, which had remained just beneath the surface against Switzerland but was now unleashed the moment the pressure was on them. It was again evident what stature Rattin possessed in midfield, now dictating to Overath and the youthful Beckenbauer. The first in danger were Germany, Weber having to clear off the line from Artimé, but at the other end Perfumo, under pressure from Seeler, headed against his own bar, and did so again not long afterwards. The physical confrontation grew harder in the second half and would have been worse but for self-restraining discipline by the Germans. Here once again was the age-old difference of interpretation: Artimé indignant at the scything tackle by which Höttges prevented him scoring, the Germans resenting the incessant off-the-ball trips, body checks and over-the-top tackles. The temperature boiled with a retaliatory foul by Overath on Gonzalez. Albrecht, Argentina's defender, who had already been cautioned for a rugby tackle on Haller, was sent off for a blatant off-the-ball foul on Weber, but against ten men Germany were

The moment he had promised to the nation. Alf Ramsey remains reflective as others react to the final whistle. Left to right; Cocker (trainer), Dr Bass, Gerry Byrne, Callaghan, Armfield, Ramsey, Flowers, Stepherdson (trainer), Greaves, Bonetti.

The squad of 27 in training at Lilleshall national recreation centre in Shropshire, before the reduction to 22 (see text). Back row (l to r): Shepherdson (trainer), Greaves, Eastham, Callaghan, Hurst, Thompson, Hunter, Gerry Byrne, Hunt, Bobby Charlton, Connelly, Milne, Springett, Armfield, Moore. Front row; Banks, McGuinness (assistant trainer), Bonetti, Flowers, Cohen, Jack Charlton, Peters, Johnny Byrne, Newton, Paine, Ball, Stiles (missing are Wilson and Tambling).

*Mexico almost succeed in smothering
England the way Uruguay did. Calderon's
fist beats Jack Charlton to the ball at a
corner – but the other Charlton would
dramatically settle the argument.*

As Pelé writhes from the double tackle by Morais, Eusebio sympathises, Americo ministrates, and the English referee McCabe absurdly strokes Dr Gosling's head.

His injured right leg strapped below the knee, Pelé vainly attempts still to contribute against Portugal.

Eusebio heads the second goal past a rooted Manga in Portugal's 3–1 victory which eliminates the champions.

Argentina quickly reveal their skill in the quarter-final against England, and Banks proves his worth as he punches clear when going up with Jack Charlton, while Peters stands by.

The temperature rises. Roma, the Argentine goal-keeper, goes down in a challenge from Jack Charlton (also fallen), and other Argentinians move in: Kreitlein, the referee, leaps to intercede.

*Rattin, the Argentinian captain, towers above
Kreitlein, and seems to be looking for witnesses in the
crowd rather than accept the signals that he must depart.*

*Argentina's ten men resolutely defy England until,
from a cross by Peters out near the left touchline, Hurst
glances a near-post header wide of Roma and inside
the far post; a classic West Ham goal.*

Top: Police, assisted by Ken Aston of the Referees' Committee, make sure that Herr Kreitlein is not troubled at the finish by Argentina autograph hunters!

An irate Ramsey attempts to prevent Cohen and Gonzalez exchanging shirts after a match which provoked England's manager to describe the opposition as animals – a remark still flying in England's face in Mexico twenty years later.

too cautious to take advantage. Argentina demonstrated the skills to compensate for being a man short, an ability they were later to confirm, in spite of FIFA's post-match warning to Lorenzo about the conduct of his players.

At Old Trafford, goals by Vutzov (an own goal), Eusebio and Torres maintained Portugal's position at the top of Group III at the expense of Bulgaria. The only goal by Chislenko, the Soviet Union's right-winger, pushed Italy into despondency at Sunderland. Rivera had been dropped, Shesternev had control of Italy's attack, and a half-hearted Italian revival following Chislenko's brilliant solo goal was thwarted by several saves by the veteran Yashin.

19 JULY. A personal record of playing in five World Cup competitions, established when the Mexicans included Carbajal in goal in place of Calderon, was the most notable fact of the goal-less draw with Uruguay at Wembley. The crowd played heroes v. villains, cheering the Mexicans if and when they showed an unexpected bit of dash, ritually booing the Uruguayans, who were all too content to settle for the draw which would give them their fourth point from only two goals scored and take them into the quarter-finals.

The crowd at Hillsborough, thick with Germans, Swiss and Yorkshiremen, united in booing the Argentinians, who inflicted Switzerland's third defeat with goals by Artimé and Onega. Rattin was the master of the match: calm, controlled and largely unadventurous in front of his rear line of defenders. The loudest cheers of the match were for the announcements of unexpected developments at Goodison and Middlesbrough.

Brazil went into their third match knowing, in the words of Dr Hilton Gosling, their chief administrator, that they were 'fighting for their lives'. They had to win by three goals against Portugal and hope that Hungary would lose the following day against Bulgaria – a slim prospect indeed. The astonishing reaction to the crisis by Feola and Gosling was to make nine changes in the team defeated by Hungary. Pelé, now fit, returned, and out went Garrincha, Santos and Bellini from the old guard. Only Lima in midfield and Jairzinho on the left wing kept their places. The strangest decisions were the recalling of the veteran Orlando in central defence, and the selection of Manga, a tall but clumsy goalkeeper, instead of Gylmar. Orlando had not played in a World Cup tie since 1958, yet such incomprehensibly muddled planning meant little to the 58,500 who came to make a comparison between Pelé and Eusebio.

Pelé was to be marked, in more than one sense, by Vincente Lucas. They had first met in a club match when Pelé was fifteen.

'I never forgot his play, and I swore he would never do the same against me again,' Lucas had said before this match. In their five subsequent encounters, Pelé had only scored twice. In the first few minutes at Goodison, Pelé, was given a flavour of what was to come when Lucas hacked him down with two uncompromising tackles from behind in the space of a few yards. George McCabe, the English referee, smiled benignly . . . and did nothing. He was a great one, McCabe, for going round patting miscreants on the head, a misguided and empty form of warning.

Manga was in trouble from almost the first move by Portugal, the ball bouncing off his chest, and from there he went downhill. After fifteen minutes, he flapped vainly at a cross from Eusebio and Simoes headed the first. Twelve minutes later Portugal were two up as Brazil's defence made only token resistance to Torres on the far post at a free kick, and his square header left Eusebio with the simplest of chances. There had already been some ill-will in the dispute for midfield possession, much of it involving Coluna, who had continued the rain of abuse on Pelé. After half an hour, it was two fouls in succession with undisguised intent by the full-back Morais, the second gouging Pelé's right leg as he staggered half-free, which put him out of the match. McCabe came across and stood looking down at Pelé without any apparent concern. Americo, Brazil's faithful old bald-headed trainer, came sprinting on to the pitch to tend his stricken god, but there was nothing in those pouches of the wide medical belt he always wore which could provide an instant cure for such brutality. Pelé was carried off, was strapped up, and returned to limp uselessly through the remainder of the match. In the second half, Rildo made it 2-1, but it was an empty gesture. Eusebio scored another, and Portugal had accomplished the demolition of the champions by methods that did them no credit – when they might well have achieved it by fair means.

A depressing aftermath of this defeat was the denigration heaped upon Pelé by some commentators, including a few of the English, who had never previously seen him and were now loudly proclaiming Eusebio as the star of the tournament. Pelé couldn't take physical challenge, they asserted, was not the man for the big occasion, was less hurt than he pretended, was always being injured. Pelé was in fact the most abused player of his time, an abuse which would subsequently be inflicted, with the compliance of inefficient referees, on Best, Cruyff and Maradona. The criticism should have been directed at the lack of action by FIFA in the face of wanton law-breaking. Marvellous goal-scorer that Eusebio was, an unforgettable sight when moving at speed and unleashing that right foot, Pelé was in my opinion much the superior player. He possessed a tactical perception, a variety and subtlety in his play which Eusebio never had, and was an even more devastating scorer of cunning goals. The Liverpool crowd which made its way home acclaiming the triumph of the man from Mozambique should have instead been lamenting the torture of a genius. Back home in Rio, the police were on guard outside Feola's house, where his wife was in physical danger in a city which had been brought to a standstill as mourners demonstrated their anger and grief. Feola elected to stay on awhile in Europe.

An equally hostile reception at home was awaiting Edmundo Fabbri, manager of Italy. He had re-instated Rivera, but in a selection upheaval little less drastic than Brazil's had retained only four of the team that had lost to the Soviet Union. After half an hour against North Korea, Bulgarelli went off with a knee injury, reducing Italy to ten men in an era without substitutes. Four minutes before half-time Pak Doo Ik, confronted by a retreating defence, had let fly to score a goal which Korea's packed defence were able to protect throughout the second half.

Fourteen Italian members of parliament tabled a question demanding to know what the government planned 'for a more dignified and moral re-organisation of the most popular sport'. The humiliating results, they claimed, had provoked a wave of national disappointment and bitterness, 'and placed the Italian sporting world in a condition of extreme embarrassment abroad'. Signor Moro, the Prime Minister, was asked to curb footballers' wages.

20 JULY. England's third match, against France, presented Henri Guérin, the French manager, with the search for a solution to a difficult equation: the need for a two-goal victory against a defence which had not yet conceded any. In training matches against Scottish amateurs – considered to be suitably physical opposition for the purpose of acclimatisation for a match with the English – France had scored twenty-seven goals in three matches. The bad news, however, had been that Eon, their first-choice goalkeeper, had broken his leg when jumping in the air to celebrate a hat-trick by Gondet, resulting in the introduction of the questionable Aubour. To get the goals, Guérin decided to switch from 4-2-4 to a 4-3-3 formation, leaving out Lucien Muller of Real Madrid and banking on a midfield of Herbin, Simon and Bonnel to get control.

A crowd of 98,000 turned up to see if they could. France suffered an early injury to Herbin, which disrupted their pattern, Herbet dropping back and Herbin returning after treatment to limp on at centre-forward. Yet with Stiles out of touch, and booked for pushing early on, France had the better of the first half-hour and England were thankful for the solidity of Jack Charlton and Moore in the centre of defence. At the other end, Hunt and Greaves were regularly caught off-side. Greaves had a goal disallowed for this, and when England went in front five minutes before half-time, the French gathered to protest that this too was off-side, never mind that Aubour had been once more at fault. A cross from Greaves on the left was headed back by Jack Charlton across the face of the goal and Hunt, suspiciously far forward, beat Aubour to the punch.

In the second half, France were still lively, keeping Cohen and Wilson busy, with Simon the driving architect of their momentum. It was therefore particularly regrettable that, after a goal by Bobby Charlton had been disallowed by Yamasaki of Peru, Hunt should head England's second through Aubour's grasp from Callaghan's cross while Simon lay in the middle of the field clutching at a leg disfigured by Stiles. This double blow finished the French and caused a furore. FIFA sent a letter to the FA, saying the disciplinary committee warned that if Stiles was reported again, either by the referee or by the official commissar appointed to attend each match, serious action would be taken. This offended everyone. Foreign critics of Stiles, who by now were legion, insisted FIFA should have taken direct action, while Ramsey justifiably regarded the letter as gross intimidation. 'Are all other players who have been cautioned also under observation from the grandstand?' he asked. Stiles was booked, of course, for pushing, not for the foul on Simon, for which he might have been sent off. He admits: 'I was aware it was late, a terrible tackle. In the last twenty minutes, I stayed out of the game. I knew it was bad. Simon used to call for the ball at throw-ins, feint to turn away, and then change direction. This time, bang, I was late, and he'd already played the ball. I couldn't apologise because that would have been hypocritcal. I knew I was wrong, and I was slated by the television panel of Danny Blanchflower, Joe Mercer and Billy Wright. Two days later, on the quiet, Alf asked me if I'd meant it. I said of course not, and he said in that case I was playing the next day in the quarter-final – "so long as you play like you did in the first seventy minutes and not the last twenty". I think he knew that I was telling the truth.'

Cohen, with a touch of indifference, says: 'It looked bloody bad, but Nobby was never wilful. I put it down to him being blind!' Stiles, who wore heavy glasses off the field, played with contact lenses. Ramsey was determined to weather the storm, as Bobby Charlton could detect. 'Alf had coated himself against outside pressures, he would not be swayed by the press or by the FA. Nothing was going to be allowed to disrupt the squad, and we would have had arguments if Nobby had been forced out.'

All Ramsey would admit publicly was a reservation about the team as a whole. I'm happy we've qualified so convincingly, but I don't think our performance in this game matched the standard in the two previous matches. There was too much casualness and it became a little irresponsible. But I had no idea the emotional pressures of the Cup would prove so severe.' What had passed unnoticed was the injury suffered by Greaves, a gash of three and a half inches through to the bone on his shin. 'I didn't know I'd done it till we'd got back in the dressing-room and I rolled my sock down and found I'd taken a chunk out. Dr Bass put five stitches in it.'

Uruguay had qualified with England and in the remaining matches elsewhere, predictable results did not stir the blood. Spain dropped their captain, Gento, had Suarez and Del Sol unfit and were beaten 2-1 at Villa Park by West Germany. Emmerich, recalled for his first appearance, scored a freak equaliser with an in-swinger from near the corner flag, and Seeler hit the winner. The Soviet Union, sure of qualifying with two victories behind them, made nine experimental changes at Sunderland and still beat Chile 2-1, in spite of Chile having more of the match. Hungary maintained the scent of former glories with a 3-1 win over Bulgaria, after being behind to an early goal by Asparoukhov.

6

South American Sulks

'NEVER, IN ANY other match, have I been kicked when the ball was at the other end as I was now. I'd look round, and one of their fellows would make a gesture of innocence! It was the worst behaviour I've ever experienced. Yet they were such a team. Terrific players. Apart from playing against them in Rio in '64, we'd seen them on TV and we considered them as difficult as anyone. I really thought it would be fifty-fifty, that they were capable of beating any team.'

Roger Hunt's opinion of England's quarter-final against Argentina would fairly represent the view of the millions of neutral people who watched a match the ill-will of which took years to subside. There can be no question that the Argentinians, who had already had Albrecht sent off and their manager and players officially warned, themselves recklessly precipitated the controversy of the match and its aftermath, at the centre of which was a short, bald, trim little tailor from Stuttgart, Rudolf Kreitlein, the referee. Following Argentina's heated exchanges on the pitch with Germany at Villa Park, the decision of FIFA to appoint a German referee for this match was naive, to say the least, and made worse by the additional appointment of Harry Cavan, the chairman of the Irish FA, as official observer. Foreigners see little national difference between London and Belfast. The fuse was lit before a ball was kicked, given the Argentinian propensity for sly and cynical fouling and the direct, robust nature of certain English players. Maybe the Argentinians would argue that, with Stiles opposing them, they were retaliating first, to adapt an expression of Danny Blanchflower's. Such a plea would convince no jury, shown the evidence.

International disapproval of Stiles had continued to rumble for the three days before the quarter-finals on 23 July. There had been, almost certainly, an abortive attempt by the FA to persuade Ramsey to leave Stiles out of his team, which was like asking Robin Hood to discard Little John, small though Stiles was.

'I think it happened at Highbury during training on Friday, the day before the match,' Stiles says. 'At one point, Alf disappeared for a while and Harold Shepherdson took over the training, which wasn't that normal, so that was probably the time. Alf had already told me I'd be playing and the next day I was ten feet tall. By Saturday, the public mood in England, especially in London, had turned in my favour, because I had my back to the wall. On the way to Wembley in the coach for the match, there were banners saying "Nobby for PM". During that match I had to be so sure of my tackles, there was so much going on you couldn't see. I was marking man-for-man on Onega, which was unusual for us, but we thought him a danger. Shepherdson and Les Cocker, the assistant trainer, had taken me on one side in the bathroom just before the match and said, "You owe Alf something, so make sure you don't let him down."'

Ramsey had made two changes from the team which beat France. Ball returned in place of Callaghan – who would not play for England again for another eleven years – and Hurst in place of Greaves, who was still recovering from his shin wound. Ball, with that self-assurance that has characterised his whole career, believes that Ramsey deliberately brought him back because he knew it was going to be hard out there. 'He didn't express any opinion about doing without a winger again, but he thought Marzolini at left-back needed watching, and it was my job to stop him coming forward. He was really hot, I had a right job to do. A winger couldn't have done it. A winger wants the ball and then to go with it. As a midfield player, I knew all about "filling in" in defence. Cally could have done it as well as me. But that match settled Alf's mind [on selection].'

The most mature man in the squad but not in the team was probably Armfield. He believes that up till this match Ramsey was not wholly sure of his best formula. 'When he announced the team, I wondered to myself if it would work. There would be a strain on the full-backs to come forward. Of course there were now two strikers who would work, and utilise the effect of Ball and Peters, with Bobby Charlton free as a "floater". Alf needed Hunt *and* Hurst for this match *physically*. It had been a bit hit-and-miss up to now. You would think a manager would play his best team from the start, but there's a bit of luck in football. Alf, mind you, was definitely not short of courage, but Hurst changed his luck. You wonder why he'd waited. With all that tension during the World Cup, I think it showed most against Argentina. Alf *knew* they were the real danger.'

In Moore's view, it wasn't so much fear as respect. 'We weren't frightened that they would beat us, but knew how difficult it would be to beat them. From all we'd seen of them we knew they were often scruffy and untidy, but that they had enormous skill, so we felt if we could beat them we could beat anybody.' England, in fact, began with a flourish, forced four corners in the first four minutes and Hurst was soon turning defenders this way and that. It was not long, either, before Argentina began to dish out the intimidation. Ball could have felt he deserved a penalty when brought down rudely by Marzolini, and the opposition was now in full swing into its ritual of chop, hack, trip and body-check to break up the opposition's game.

Yet Argentina, all too obviously, could pose threats of a more legitimate nature. A cross headed away by Jack Charlton flew straight to Mas. The heavily muscled little winger swung and his fierce half-volley all but got the better of Banks. Throwing himself down full length, Banks managed to scuffle the ball out from just inside the left-hand post. England were not innocent in the tenacious disputes for the ball, and over the course of the match were penalised thirty-three times compared with the nineteen fouls awarded against Argentina. But England's excess was in challenges directly for the ball, and regarded as legitimate attempts under the European interpretation of the laws. There could be no such licence granted to the clear intent of the Argentinians, and within a short time Perfumo and Solari had been booked by Kreitlein, whose 'fussiness' had more to do with his manner than his decisions.

Rattin, stooping, round-shouldered and hawk-faced, was playing with every particle of his exceptional skills, controlling and passing the ball more deftly than anyone on the pitch and all the time without breaking into more than a trot. Infuriatingly, he also fouled without compunction almost any time he lost the ball. When, just after the half-hour, Bobby Charlton swayed past him, Rattin ruthlessly up-ended him, and in spite of having his name taken was soon giving the same treatment to Hunt. When, a moment later, Artimé had his name taken, Rattin attempted to protest, standing over Kreitlein like a schoolmaster berating a small boy.

The England players are almost unanimous that Rattin, by his constant fouling and arguing, now pushed Kreitlein's patience beyond the point of endurance. 'He never left the ref alone, and he stopped him keeping up with the game,' Bobby Charlton says. 'It was certain the ref would have to do something.' Cohen echoes this: 'Rattin was going on at the ref all the time, he tried to run the game. But what a bloody good player he was! If we'd wanted to get rid of anyone, it would certainly have been him. I had looked forward to the chance of perhaps playing the Hungarians, but the Argentinians were very negative. Then suddenly they'd *go*. There was a great need for your awareness at any moment when they didn't seem concerned.'

As Rattin stood gesticulating, and drawing Kreitlein's attention to his captain's arm-band, the rest of the Argentinians gathered around them. Albrecht, who had served his one-match suspension for being sent off against West Germany, now tried to lead off the entire team. The whole group, all arguing, gradually moved to the side of the pitch, with Kreitlein almost obscured from view by the swarm of pale blue-and-white striped shirts. Now they were joined by Lorenzo, from the bench, and the other team attendants, plus Cavan and Ken Aston, the chairman of the referees' committee who had been the man at the centre of the Chile-Italy rumpus in 1962. With Kreitlein insistently waving, with a short flick of the wrist like some conductor, that Rattin must depart, and with Rattin equally in no mood to comply, it seemed that the match might well have to be abandoned. At one point a conciliatory Wilson joined the group and said: 'Let him off, ref, and let's get on with the shambles.'

With eventually the police intervening in order to segregate Rattin from his colleagues, it took some eight minutes to achieve a return to normality. It was a hot afternoon, and England utilised the interlude to have a sponge-down with Shepherdson. As play re-started, Rattin, the first man ever to be sent off at Wembley, made a slow and provocative walk around the side of the pitch to the tunnel. There was more conflict on the pitch as Hurst made a disgracefully high tackle on Ferreiro, for which he was fortunate not to be made to join Rattin – he was probably saved by Ferreiro's histrionic reaction to the offence. Half-time came as a merciful rest.

It was widely assumed that England would proceed to exploit Argentina's numerical handicap without too much difficulty in the second half. With grudging praise, the crowd were obliged to acknowledge the outstanding football sense and skills of Argentina, as they continued to match the home team stride for stride, with a performance which belatedly revealed what they might have inflicted on England had they exercised some self-discipline from the start. The second half began with a wonderful save by Roma, who leaped high to turn a ferocious shot by Hurst over the bar. Onega had taken over from Rattin in midfield and showed the ability of the instinctive footballer, such as Peters, to play in any position. Onega held Argentina together to the extent that Mas and Artimé, supported by Ferreiro and Marzolini from full-back, were able to generate sufficient attacking moves still to have won the game. It seemed, indeed, that extra time or even a reply might be forced, such was Argentina's imaginative resilience. Then came that decisive moment, a combination of judgement and long club experience, for which Ramsey's selection of the team might be deemed discerning, or lucky. Wilson pushed a conventional pass down the left to Peters, who without looking up turned inside and curled an away-swinging cross into space to the left of the corner of the six-yard area. There on the end of it was the soaring figure of Hurst, who, with a perfectly judged flick of which Tommy Lawton would have been proud, glanced the ball beyond Roma and into the far side of the net. In that moment, internationally, Geoff Hurst had arrived: though he had more in store for us.

'We'd worked on near-post goals till it became an automatic action,' Peters recalls. 'I wouldn't even have to look. Up till then, Argentina had played sensibly in the second half and we'd had difficulty getting the ball off them even with only ten men. Then, following a throw-in, I think, I was left unmarked for the first time. I was in open space when I got the ball from Ray, and quickly knocked it in. I knew Geoff would be there, it was only a matter of hitting the right height, curling it a bit. In previous matches, I wouldn't even think of hitting balls in there like that unless Geoff was playing. In later years, I developed the same relationship at Tottenham with Martin Chivers.'

Before the finish, Mas had one chance to level the score but Banks was equal to it, and the match ended with Argentina knowing that, as much as by Hurst's goal, they had been eliminated by their own, habitual, indiscipline. 'They were the best side we met,' Ball says. 'We'd wanted to get on with it from the start, to play them at football, but their shirt-pulling and everything broke our rhythm and drove some of us to do things we wouldn't ordinarily do. They were clever, and as Ray Wilson says, even when they had ten men you could count on one hand the times we got round behind them.' The arguments surrounding Kreitlein continued for days: indeed until the present time among football people. It was said he would have been justified in bringing charges for assault against one or two Argentinians for what happened during the eight-minute delay. The following day Kreitlein defended his action when he said: 'I had taken Rattin's name once, and then cautioned him. He said nothing I could understand, but I could read in his face what he was saying. He was following me around the field shouting at me, but although he towered over me I was not afraid of him. I had no alternative but to send him off. This was undoubtedly the roughest game I had handled in twenty years.'

Kreitlein was condemned by some for the extreme and unique action of sending a man off for the look in his eye. Hunt thinks that Rattin was unlucky to be made to go. 'He wasn't fouling more than anyone else, and arguing with the referee is an accepted part of the game in South America.' Therein lies the controversy over the matter of interpretation, but my own opinion, then and now, having watched a re-run on television, is that Rattin's behaviour amounted to deliberate attempted intimidation of the referee, quite apart from his own fouling, and that Kreitlein had no alternative. FIFA took the same attitude.

Argentina were fined 1,000 Swiss francs, the maximum permitted (then about £80), and threatened with exclusion from the next World Cup. Rattin was suspended for the next four international matches, Ferreiro and Onega for the next three. Argentina's reaction was predictably emotional. Dr Menendez Behety, an official of their federation, said: 'The referee was biased and provoked our players,' an opinion which overlooked the fact that Kreitlein gave fourteen more free kicks against England than Argentina.

Argentinian television, in analysing the row, highlighted the difference of interpretation when a commentator claimed: 'We think it is less wrong to argue with the referee than to kick an opponent when tackling from behind, even if going for the ball. And it *always* takes five minutes to send a player off in Argentina.'

As the players had left the field at the finish, an irate Ramsey had physically prevented Cohen from exchanging shirts with Gonzalez, and later on television had said in an interview: 'We had still to produce our best football. It will come against the right kind of opposition, a team who come out to play football and not act like animals.' For this indiscretion, FIFA's disciplinary committee wrote to the FA demanding that they should caution their manager about his future behaviour.

Back at the Hendon Hall Hotel that evening Ramsey allowed the squad to let their hair down. Stiles recalls: 'We all got well and truly drunk, just the lads, and Alf was sat over there in the corner and never said a word.' The players knew they had cleared their biggest hurdle. 'Argentina had the best defence in the competition, their back people were superb, big and strong and confident,' Bobby Charlton says. '*They* believed they were going to win it [the Cup], but they were a bit frightened of us and needed to break us down, intimidating, not allowing us to play. If you pushed the ball past them, they'd always check you, stop you at all costs. Yet they were such good players.' Jack, in defence, felt less concerned at the time. 'They didn't cause us too much trouble at the back. Once, early on, that little fellow [Mas] had a whack, but Gordon saved. It was the only time. Rattin was incredible, kicking people, always yapping, always on at the ref. I remember thinking, "Why don't they get on with the game?" When Rattin was sent off, they mainly defended.'

Wilson pin-points the inherent conflict of the two teams' styles. 'They'd won in '64 in Rio without conceding a goal, so we knew they'd be difficult to play against. Theirs was a waiting game, and *we* were a counter-punching team. So the home team needed to change its style a bit. We were fortunate to have Geoff in the side. Until we had him, we couldn't play a fifty-fifty ball up front to draw a defender, because you need a big man, good in the air, so that you can profit from knock-downs.'

The Peters-Hurst goal was a turning point of the competition. 'Looking back, you realise how certain units function together,' Moore says. 'Nobby and Bobby Charlton were from United; Geoff, Martin and me from West Ham. That was half the team. It was so important to our operation. The most critical goal we might never have got other than with West Ham's background, and that's not being disrespectful to other clubs and players.' Jack Charlton reflects: 'As a manager, Alf always liked balance. Martin Peters was a mainly right-footed person, so when he came in I had doubts – were we balanced? But it didn't matter, Martin was always sneaking in, getting behind opponents into the box. He was a good passer, very rarely gave the ball away. The one-touch football at times was tremendous, with men like Peters and Ball, it made them so difficult to mark.'

The goal posed a major problem for one Englishman: Greaves. 'There was no way I could have been fit for that match, there was a bit of infection in the wound, and it was touch and go whether I'd be ready for the final,' he says. 'I knew, honestly, after Argentina, that unless someone was injured my chance of getting back was questionable. Geoff had that goal, Roger had been Roger, doing his job, though nothing outstanding. With no substitutes, I guessed my chance had probably gone.'

If it had been an ugly day at Wembley, it had been little better up at Roker Park in Sunderland, where West Germany had defeated Uruguay 4-0, but only after the Latin Americans had two men sent off in the second half . . . by Jim Finney, an English referee. It was no surprise if that evening there were dark allegations by the South American participants in the competition – bearing in mind McCabe's lenience towards Portugal – that there was a conspiracy between Sir Stanley Rous and FIFA in favour of Europe.

The match was orderly enough for the first half. Beckenbauer was playing a more liberated role than hitherto, often moving into attack. There was even more of a contrast in styles than at Wembley, between the fast-raiding Held and Emmerich and the slow, suddenly explosive tactics of Uruguay. The only goal in the first half came against the run of play. Held, evading two tackles, hit a speculative shot which glanced off Haller and gave Mazurkieviez in goal no chance.

Germany had to thank Tilkowski for saving from Salva and Rocha, and half-time arrived with it still being anybody's match in a fascinating duel of differing techniques. At the start of the second half, Germany gained an initiative and it was now that Uruguay started fouling at random. Cortes was cautioned and when Troche, the captain and sweeper, put his knee into Emmerich, out of sight of Mr Finney but clearly seen by a linesman, he was inevitably sent off, slapping Seeler in the face for good measure as he departed. Barely had this happened when Haller was cynically felled by Silva, and he too was dismissed. Like Rattin at Wembley, he required the persuasion of police to convince him that Mr Finney was in earnest. Reduced to nine men and already one down, Uruguay were without hope. Their despairing response to their situation was to attack, which duly provided Germany with the space to score another three. Beckenbauer walked the ball round the goalkeeper, and Seeler and Haller got the other two. As the teams departed down the tunnel for the dressing-rooms, Cortes kicked Finney, for which he was suspended for six months. Troche and Silva were suspended for three matches.

'It's always difficult to play against South Americans when they don't win!' Helmut Schoen said philosophically. 'There is no middle ground to their game or their temperament. They are either up or down. Their mentality plays a great part in their results. Europeans therefore always like to do the things which are not there in the South American game. Otherwise the South Americans will overwhelm them with technique. It may have helped when Troche was sent off, but our confidence was growing at that time, and we were in a good mood. They complained afterwards about Silva – the *severity* – but a referee has to decide in that moment. A good team always depends on personalities, positive within their own side and negative towards the opposition. But you can't have too many negative players, as the South Americans sometimes have, too many players who want to show what they can do with the ball. A successful team needs one or two strong, unselfish players, like Hunt for England. Eddie Merckx, the famous Belgian cyclist, would never have won all his races without the support of colleagues who nobody remembers now. Our strongest and also most unselfish personality was Seeler, our captain.'

The South American Confederation issued a statement in London that the threatened ban on Argentina was not within the jurisdiction of the disciplinary committee, and that the committee should have taken action on Ramsey and not passed responsibility to the FA; and then they went home in a huff for an executive meeting in Buenos Aires in September, 'to examine the difficulties faced by Brazil, Argentina, Uruguay and Chile in the finals'. One man who was in no doubt about recognising the difficulties, and the need to attempt to eradicate a self-inflicted ailment, was Cesar Luiz Menotti, who twelve years later would guide Argentina to victory having worked tirelessly to convince his players that violence was not a necessary ingredient of victory.

In the quarter-final at Goodison, the fluctuations of a remarkable match, which Portugal won 5-3 after being three down to North Korea, told us more about a suspect Portuguese defence than any oriental wizardry. Pak Seung Zin, Li Dong Woon and Yang Sung Kook took advantage, to the incredulity of television and radio commentators, of Korea passing the ball consistently to their own shirts instead of the Portuguese. When Portugal finally woke up, they were fortunate to have Eusebio to undo the damage: he scored four, including two penalties, and made the cross from which Augusto scored the fifth.

Before their match with the Soviet Union, the Hungarians had been boasting about what they might do should they play their hosts. 'If we play England, Stiles won't know the game is played with a ball, he'll never get near enough to touch it,' Bené had said. They never got the chance. Hungary were without a win over their Russian political masters since the halcyon days of Puskas and Hidegkuti, and now they were miserably undermined once more in this competition by the dearth of a reliable goalkeeper. After five minutes at Hillsborough, Gelei dropped a shot from Malofeev straight at the feet of Chislenko for the simplest of goals. The Russian defence matched Rakosi's speed down the left flank, Khusainov and Sabo controlled the middle of the field, and Yashin was seldom called upon after a valuable save from Sipos in the thirty-eighth minute. Two minutes after half-time Porkujan, unmarked, scored a second and Bené's reply came too late for a revival. Brilliant, thrilling Hungary had foundered.

7

Wingless Wonders

ANY PUBLIC RELATIONS company trying to promote the good name of the World Cup would, after the quarter-finals, have been approaching the point of nervous breakdown. The competition was running at the rate of a foul every three minutes: some 850 fouls in 2,520 minutes of twenty-eight matches. In a strident article in the *Daily Mail*, their columnist Jim Manning thundered: 'What has happened to sport is what has already happened to people.' There were those who wondered whether FIFA had noticed: or even cared.

At a government reception at Lancaster House for those eliminated in the first round, Joao Havelange, chairman of the Brazilian federation and later to depose Rous as president of FIFA, had said: 'Never again would I allow Pelé to play in the World Cup after the treatment he has received in this competition. It is the pointless sacrifice of a great player. If this is how football is to be played, then we must select players with less skill and stronger physique, however much we may regret such action. After this, Pelé can play in exhibition or friendly matches, when we can put on a substitute, but in the World Cup we can no longer afford the risk of having to play with ten men.' Pelé, meanwhile, was signing autographs on five-pound notes for fellow players who recognised the privilege of being a contemporary. Pelé would, of course, play a notable part in Brazil's recovery and triumph four years later, by which time substitution had been approved. Sadly, when Havelange himself became president, he would show no such sensitively protective attitude towards the great players of other countries, such as Maradona, when they were subjected to similar wanton intimidation.

McCabe, the English referee in charge in the match when Pelé was injured by Portugal, was eliminated from subsequent matches in 1966. Sir Walter Winterbottom, who at various times was a member of FIFA's advisory technical committee, says: 'It was most unfortunate that Pelé should catch two such tackles within a few feet. Riding the first, he had no chance with the second. It is essential for referees to book players early in the game for deliberate fouls on star players.' When Schumacher of West Germany kicked Battiston of France almost to death in the 1982 semi-final, FIFA simply closed its eyes.

Yet the world game in 1966 was being confused by more than just foul tactics. Some of the legitimate play was causing no less consternation, not least England's. Part of the problem was that conventions for describing players' positions, and the shirt numbers which they wore, were now being disrupted so that spectators and commentators could no longer be precisely sure of what they were looking at. Those reminiscing in the office, factory, pub or home could no longer slip into customary definitions. There was a new jargon, which new young pro-fessional coaches would exercise in a pretence that they knew more about the game than they really did. Centre-forwards had become strikers, inside-forwards and wing-halves had become link-men or midfielders, wingers played 'wide', centre-halves were now centre-backs. No doubt this was all a necessary adjustment to what was happening on the field. The description 'deep-lying centre-forward' was indeed inadequate for the role so deceptively filled ten years before by Hidegkuti, and later by Revie and Johnny Byrne. But as a result of this development, spectators were more than ever being pushed into the status of outsiders. Simultaneously, the players upon whom they lavished their admiration, such as Greaves, were under threat from the new attitudes of coaches. It was significant, for example, that Edmundo Fabbri, Italy's manager, saw fit to drop the cleverest player in the country, Rivera, while the explosive Corso of Internazionale was not even in the squad of twenty-two because, like Thompson of Liverpool, he was 'too unpredictable'.

I was one of the few who consistently supported Ramsey's policies for the first eight years of his management, because I believed them to be effective and not necessarily lacking in entertainment. The trouble was that Ramsey's premise was to create a team which, first and foremost, was difficult to beat. Such thinking is hardly original. Herbert Chapman had done the same forty years before. Ramsey was carrying it a stage further, and it was the work of pale imitators, hoping to achieve similar success with his system but with less understanding, who would lead the game into a downward and ultimately irreversible trend. The fact that England had fallen short of brilliance in their first four matches was not in itself justification for criticism. Had not Brazil scrambled through some of their early matches in 1958, notably against England (0-0) and Wales (1-0), and again in 1962?

Before the tournament began it had been obvious that what would determine the outcome was not so much England's capacity for greatness, which was marginal, as the ability of anyone to beat them, which was problematic, in the light of only one defeat in twenty-one matches. Yet Pelé, taking a philosophic view of the new tactics, which required an increasing number of defenders by the pulling back, or conversion, of forwards who would need more stamina, said when we discussed the issue: 'The players you are developing in England will not last at the top for more than a few years. They will burn out, have too many injuries. There will never be a team like Brazil's, to dominate world football for eight to ten years, because players won't survive. No England team would win most of its matches in South America the way we have in Europe. Ideal football has become impossible. This is terrible for the game and the spectators, who want a show. This has been obvious with your English crowd, especially in Manchester and Liverpool. They are not as fanatical as at home, but more discerning. They have appreciated good football, whatever the team. From what I have seen, only two teams, Brazil and Hungary, have played attacking football. Only by allowing the other team to attack can you do so yourselves. The present negative trend chokes all this. There are only two ways to beat it – by playing the same way, or having better referees.' It was the best analysis I had heard, and a reflection of it may be found in the enduring attitude of West Ham.

Most teams were being tempted to compromise their natural instincts. Helmut Schoen said: 'I think Argentina and Uruguay at this time came to believe they had to have a more physical condition and approach, and in consequence lost some of their technical advantage. They lost their true direction, their typical game.' It was, however, undeniable that three teams notable for their organisation, England, West Germany and the Soviet Union, had reached the semi-finals and inevitably this would persuade coaches to re-think the gospel. Sepp Herberger, Germany's manager when they won the Cup in 1954 and who had handed over to Schoen in 1963, was an observer of the 1966 finals, and defended the tactics of the Europeans. 'The South Americans are too much in love with the ball, they embroider too much,' he said. 'Argentina had the ability, but England are justified in reaching the semi-final. As a team they have no weakness, which is rare. My criticism is that they develop counter-attacks so fast, with its surprise element, they do not give themselves time to regroup and support the front player who has the ball.'

This was a complimentary and accurate assessment of Ramsey's team. In the last five pre-World Cup matches against foreign opposition at home, and now in the recent four, there had been an encouraging number of openings created, but many wasted: a profusion of method, but an absence of rhythm. Part of the pressure on Ramsey was the need to find alternative ways of playing because of a decline, which would only become really evident in later years, in instinctive ability. There were available to him three styles of play: with the wingers, as employed by West Germany and Portugal; with collective groups of players moving in fast inter-changing attack, as used by Hungary, Brazil and, to a degree when brave enough, Italy; and counter-attacking from midfield, as used by England and the South Americans, England doing so with more persistence and energy.

Ramsey was not, as his detractors insisted then and to this day, *against* wingers. He had used three, Connelly, Paine and Callaghan, in the first three matches. The truth about Thompson was that in sixteen internationals he had not scored a single goal. By contrast Peters, brought in on the left, would score twenty goals in his sixty-seven internationals and is still England's twelfth highest scorer of all time. Greaves reflects: 'I had the feeling when Alf took over that he was very meticulous, and I recognised straight away that he would find it difficult to fit in someone like me. I think he realised I could do a job, but I wasn't his kind of player.' Those seeking to simplify the issue merely asserted that Ramsey mistrusted genius when it did not come dripping in sweat, but that was to underestimate Ramsey's intelligence.

Wilson says that from a full-back's point of view it was much easier in the simple confrontation of the old WM formation. 'I much preferred to play against a winger, a personal battle,' he says. 'In the old days, wingers never went back much over the half-way line, and I remember playing against Ireland when they put Jimmy McIlroy, who was a conventional inside-forward with Burnley, on the field in a No. 7 shirt. But of course he wasn't a winger at all in that match, and he soon disappeared, making it really difficult for me. I remember looking at the Spanish right-back in Madrid, when we first played 4-3-3, and he was totally confused who to mark. In the next few years, as everyone copied England's system, I found it made *my* life harder. Alf's answer to other people doing this was zonal marking, picking people up as they moved into your area, but that is very difficult at a lower level of the game, and you've got to be playing together for a long time for it to be effective.'

Connelly agrees that with the increase in massed defences, the winger's job became impossible. He says: 'You now have to have people breaking from midfield, like Bobby Charlton or Martin.

The sort of traditional front-running I was supposed to do just wasn't on. Everywhere you went, you were running into a defender. Other managers, trying to copy Alf's plan, didn't understand it. A winger can't repeatedly work from one eighteen-yard line to the other, and still have the sharpness to do his job. When Alf played me, he didn't want me back, he wanted me wide on either flank, and I got nearly all my international goals playing with him. That was what I knew. We always played with two wingers at Burnley: Pilkington, Harris, myself, Coates, Kindon – and Alf wanted you to do what you knew. When he left me out after the Uruguay match and brought back Peters, he said on the bus, "Don't think I'm being unfair with you, you had a good run, but I want to try something else." If the goals had gone in then, maybe we'd have stayed the same.'

Bobby Charlton, two years younger than I, and my idol in my apprentice days as a journalist when still retaining fading ambitions as an amateur international, was one of the most exciting wingers I ever saw: fast, with a marvellous body swerve, and unbelievable power in either foot. Although it was as an inside-forward that he first came to national attention in the FA Cup Final of 1957, much of his early international career was spent on the left wing, where he scored 24 of his 49 goals before Ramsey switched him inside. He gave spectators a tingling expectation that, like some fictional hero of the *Wizard,* so long as he was still running, England always had a chance of victory. Yet he admits to reservations about the role. 'When I played on the wing for England I disliked it, because I depended so much on other players to get the ball. When you move into midfield, you're active all the time, you're in the game. On the other hand, after playing inside-forward or midfield, it's easier playing on the wing. You get more room to do things. The way we played in '66, you had to have discipline as well as skill, you had to have fit players. The legacy was that everyone afterwards thought, "That's the way to play," but overlooked the fact that you need good players. So Alf was crucified, but it wasn't his fault.'

Two essentials of Ramsey's eventual formation were the versatility of Ball and Peters, and the use of Stiles as a plug in front of the defence, who would win the ball and then hand it on to creative players. Cohen feels football became less enjoyable on account of the changes but accepts the rationale. 'Obviously Alf didn't think the wingers who were available were good enough. The commentators called us "wingless wonders", but the open spaces on the pitch were still there. If English football has gone down the pan, it's because managers and coaches haven't had the intelligence to understand what they were doing. Personally, I found it boring not to play against a winger as a full-back, but with someone like Martin, you could *see* him thinking, always arriving at the right time. He was never static, always coming off the ball. Nobby was great around our penalty area, a policeman . . . he could tackle a tank.'

Any judgement of Stiles is complicated by the amiability of this controversial little player off the field. He was, and is, a thoroughly decent fellow, popular with his colleagues and the spirited kind of person who helps to cement the morale and good humour of a squad. On the field, without question, he was provocative. He says, for instance, that against Argentina he had to be careful with his tackling on account of his warning from FIFA. Ought he not to have been more careful at all times?

Nobody would wish the character of football to be enfeebled by taking away its robust physical contact, which has always been there and gives it that underlying need for courage. The western Europeans have always tended to have a more brazen kind of physical courage, the British most of all, committing themselves in a way which often puts them at as much risk as the opponent they flinch. The Latin, by comparison, tends to be more subtle or even, at times, sly, confining his violence to moments when his attention is not distracted by the ball and the opponent is off guard. The British have tended to carry what they regard as legitimate challenges for the ball, even from the side or from behind, to an extreme. They have accepted that it is allowable to go through an opponent's legs if ultimately you come away with the ball, which makes nonsense of the legitimate skill of the Latin or Slav – or indeed of such players as George Best, Charlie Cooke and John White – in shielding the ball by the positioning of their legs and body. There had always been physical players in British football such as Tommy Banks, the Bolton full-back, Jimmy Scoular, the Newcastle wing-half, and Dave Mackay of Spurs. There can be little doubt that Duncan Edwards, that young lion of Manchester United, would have been increasingly involved in controversy for his tackling of foreigners had he survived the Munich crash. What was different about Stiles, and that school of destructive midfield and defensive players who were to dominate the next twenty years, was that, through supreme fitness and application, they were never more than a couple of strides away from an opponent, and were able to challenge for the ball at the very moment the opponent received the ball rather than after he had got it under control. This caused a rise in frustration and the level of temper on the part of creative players who were being suppressed: viz, Gentile of Italy.

Bobby Charlton defends Stiles like a brother: which on the pitch he was. Stiles, he says in defiance of some of the evidence, was not dirty. 'Nobby was a bloody nuisance, always there, and never overawed by anyone's reputation,' Bobby insists. 'He did a job, and he was an underrated player. He was picked for English schoolboys because he was creative, not for his tackling. Mind you, he was accident-prone. When he had a minor bump in his car, he split his head open on the other driver's head bending down to look at the damage. He'd lose his car keys, and find they were in the ignition. Things were always happening to him, off the field.'

Stiles, then and now, was undismayed by his reputation, and not surprisingly puts some of the responsibility for his attitude on the pitch upon Jimmy Murphy, that resolute assistant at Old Trafford and manager of Wales, alongside whom Matt Busby could always play the gentleman. Murphy was not above encouraging Stiles to put an opponent in the first row of the stand. 'If I wasn't jeered at and booed, I considered I wasn't doing my job,' Stiles says with a frankness which is alarming. 'With England, I was there to protect Bobby [Charlton], to win the ball. After that, if there was a white shirt, pass to it. It sounds easy, but people forget what my responsibility was. I was there to read the situation early. Our formation was in fact 4-1-3-2, with me playing in front of the back four and behind Ball, Charlton and Peters, with Hurst and Hunt up front. I was quick, and a good tackler, but my role was different to what it was with United, where I played at the back with Bill Foulkes.

'I remember when the system first changed from the old WM formation, with one wing-half more on attack, the other more defensive. When Crerand arrived at Old Trafford as an attacking wing-half, Setters became more defensive. I realised *that* was the job I could do. In 1964, Setters was injured, and I played against Greaves in London. I knew that if I did okay that day, it would be doubly good. For me, that was the turning-point. You've got to have luck, and that was mine. There were players better than me with United, players like Brennan and Dunne, who aren't remembered, but I was. I'll be remembered as the villain, but people under-estimated me.

'Although I was small, I was afraid of no one. With bigger fellows, I could knock them over because I was better balanced. But I wasn't like that off the field. It made me smile when a women's magazine, interviewing my wife [Kay, the sister of Johnny Giles], asked her whether I beat her! I was more worried about the effect of my reputation on my parents, but I don't think it upset them.'

Stiles acknowledges that, after 1966, things at times got worse rather than better, that he heard managers and trainers exhorting their players from the bench to do damage on men such as George Best. This was the new face of football, where those with ability had to be stifled. Yet it could not be said that Ramsey's attitude was one of destruction, whatever his loyalty to Stiles. His most positive contribution to the principles of international team selection, which Revie, Greenwood, Robson and Taylor have failed to follow or been unable to because of injuries, was of continuity. 'You just cannot keep altering an international team,' Jack Charlton says. 'Players are always having to make allowances for the strengths and weaknesses of others, and if the team keeps changing, nobody gets to know what these are. What Alf did was to introduce a fluid way to play, which allowed Bobby to run, and Ball, but still meant you could get people back very quickly. An outstanding relationship was between Nobby, Bobby Moore and myself. Nobby was always between us and the ball and took some of the pressure off us. You can't say whether our style of playing did harm to the game. The game today is more hustling, more closing down of areas. Alf was a stickler for not giving the ball away, always saying our passing had got to be better, to keep possession. It was the same at Leeds, where we used to say they couldn't get the ball away from us. We killed them. I've always been a believer in central midfield ball-winners in front of the back four, it stops the back four getting dragged about. It started at Leeds with Collins, and Nobby was the same for England.'

Jack Charlton is, of course, one of the most responsible-minded contemporary coaches in Britain, but it is significant that when he talks of killing time it must also unavoidably mean the killing of spectator interest for any but a home crowd.

Martin Peters epitomised the changes which were taking place in the game under Ramsey's leadership, and it is a contradiction that while Peters learned his football with West Ham, who have retained a comparatively high level of popularity with their inventive and open football, the game as a whole has for thirty years declined. Peters was that rarity, a great player who was not fully appreciated by the majority of those who saw him, because of his subtlety. Ramsey described him in 1968 as a player 'ten years ahead of his time'; which was not only a tribute but an indication of Ramsey's foresight: for this was several years ahead of the emergence of the 'total football' of Holland and West Germany which was to establish a further change in tactical precepts. If football is a synthesis of war, chess and ballet, Peters provided the chess. For that he owes something to Greenwood. 'I'd been at West Ham two years when Ron arrived, but with him we did a lot on *awareness, where* the ball should be played, the tactics. It was being a West Ham player that made you able to modify yourself, to switch positions as Geoff did from wing-half to centre-forward. People forget that in the '65 Cup Winners final with Munich, Geoff played in midfield between me and Boyce, behind two wingers and a centre-forward, Sissons-Dear-Seeley. Alf never said a lot about my style. Maybe with that label he gave me, "ten years", he tried to give me more of an identity.'

Ball, the other ersatz winger, was as different from Peters as chalk from cheese: a hustler who thrived on direct involvement, could win the ball, and loved to dribble. Though he sometimes lacked the speed to carry him clear, at the same time he was a superb first-time passer of the ball through any sort of angle. If he lacked Peters's subtlety or his goal-scoring ability – eight goals in seventy-two appearances – he inflicted as much damage on the opposition's confidence by unrelenting will-power. If such is possible, he was even more competitive than Stiles, and occasionally this would get him into trouble, too. 'Nobby and I died so that Bobby could live,' he says. 'Bobby was different, a world-class player. Nobby and me were there to give him the ball, to give him time. It taught me there is room for this quality in a team. Bobby Charlton thought that "tackle" was what you go fishing with.'

Armfield pays tribute to the contribution of Ball, his colleague at Blackpool; to what, by the semi-final, was now an outstanding team. 'Ball reached his best in the World Cup: ambitious and energetic. Peters and Ball gave their team their "legitimacy" on the outside of the pitch. Bobby Charlton was the trump, who allowed them to play that system. Playing 4-3-3, you need someone as mobile. He was our Pelé or Beckenbauer.'

Franz Beckenbauer says how difficult the new system was for any opposition. 'Alf Ramsey was the first coach to play without wingers, and with two strikers in the middle, and making space for the midfielders and the full-backs, Cohen and Wilson, to run forward and create a lot of problems. This system was unique at the time because almost everybody played with wingers, so our team and others found it hard to do anything against this, because the system was strange for them. I think it was this system that won the World Cup for England.'

Jimmy Greaves sounds the lament. 'Everyone got embroiled in the system, even Bill Nicholson at Tottenham. Individual players like me became "luxuries". Now, it was all *systems*. It was the downfall of the game. The people I feel sorry for are those who came along like Rodney Marsh and Stan Bowles, great individuals, who were frowned upon. They were rejected in favour of the automaton.'

8

'Everything You Want'

26/27 JULY   THE COMMISSIONNAIRE who was letting out the VIP guests at the directors' entrance at Goodison Park, after the first, and boring, semi-final between West Germany and the Soviet Union, was almost apologetic. 'I can tell you,' he confided with a bit of a sigh, 'neither of those two would beat Everton's reserves.' At that time, regularly drawing crowds of several thousand, Everton's reserves were an attractive team, as Trebilcock had recently proved on his promotion to the Cup Final side, and the truth was that these World Cup contenders had given us the very worst kind of semi-final: cautious, negative and often dirty. It was further evidence that when intelligent tactics are mutually neutralising, the entertainment level is usually low.

Schoen made no apologies twenty years later. He felt that the characteristics of the two sides were always likely to produce a spectacle which would disappoint the public appetite. 'We'd watched Russia in the earlier rounds, and we didn't fear them. We had no special plan for this match, merely to play our own game. Russia were not at the same level of world football so much at that time, and I thought that we would beat them on the evidence that we had. Being close to the final, it would be unreasonable to expect us to be the adventurous team when we knew that Russia had been consistently hard up till now, and that we were likely to find ourselves in a physically tough game.'

The crowd was a disappointing 38,000, a reflection of Merseyside's disillusionment with FIFA's decision to alter its intention, and stage England's semi-final in London rather than the north west. It was said that the reason was financial, to utilise the larger capacity of Wembley, which of course would be a sell-out with England playing. Not only was such expediency of questionable football ethics, increasing the allegations of favouritism towards the hosts, but it was an insult to the enthusiasm and appreciation which Liverpudlians had demonstrated in substantial numbers towards several of the foreign guests. Not to permit them to see an England team, six of whom were from the north, was a failure in public relations. There can be little doubt that Ramsey's men would have responded with a natural allegiance to a crowd of their ethnic followers, and would have had a chance to demonstrate that their abilities were not confined to Wembley.

With Höttges injured, Germany had to bring in Lutz at right-back. The Soviet Union were not without their skilful players, notably Voronin, Chislenko and Banishevsky, but they were quickly into their intimidating stride as Danilov brought down Seeler, as a result of which Germany's captain spent the next twenty minutes limping. The veteran Yashin maintained his rivalry to Banks as the best goalkeeper in the tournament with a breath-taking save from Emmerich, who thereafter had one of his anonymous spells and faded from the game. Germany were by now responding to the Soviet challenge to see whose bones were harder and whose courage the steadier. Sabo was hurt when he himself tried to raise the temperature. Such football as there was to be seen came mainly from the Germans, Beckenbauer and Overath trying to open avenues and Seeler, now recovering, probing the Russians with those bustling runs. Yashin had to summon all his experience and judgement to make one of the best saves of the tournament from Seeler. Voronin, for all his poise, became entangled in the ugly mood and had his name taken.

Germany, whom history has shown to be reluctant victims, were matching anything that was thrown at them in the matter of studs, and it was from a ferocious tackle by Schnellinger two minutes before half-time that Germany's first goal stemmed. Removing the ball from Chislenko as though in a smash and grab raid, he then raced for the Russian penalty area. A sharp pass across the face of the goal found Haller, and his first-time, right-footed shot was too much for Yashin. The doubtful legitimacy of Schnellinger's tackle hung heavily on Chislenko's mind, and a minute later in delayed retaliation he hurled himself at Held and hammered him to the ground. His sending off by Lo Bello of Italy was unavoidable, and thus Russia's set-back had been doubled at a stroke; the more so as, when they left the field for the interval, Sabo was seen to be limping heavily.

The situation should have been tailor-made for Germany's creative players to dispose of Russia's nine and a half men with a flourish in the second half, but they disappointingly failed to do so, encouraging the spectators to begin derisively chanting

'England'. Though nobody neutral by now cared much about the result, it was put beyond doubt with some twenty-five minutes to go with a superb goal by young Beckenbauer. A drive by Overath was turned away by Yashin for a corner, from which Emmerich hit an out-swinger. Beckenbauer, controlling the ball perfectly, gave himself sight of the goal by drifting wide of a group of defenders and smashed home a superb shot. By the time Porkujan scored late in the game, many of the spectators were on their way home. Better things were expected from England and Portugal the following day, and expectation was to be fulfilled, albeit in London.

'We had respect for Portugal, but were confident we would win,' Bobby Charlton says. 'In fact, they were stronger in the semi-final than we expected. I'd felt there was no one who was likely to score against us. I bet none of the teams who played us *enjoyed* it. We were full of runners, we got back, we made the other team *work*.' It is indicative of the mood of Ramsey's squad that their most exhilarating player was himself conditioned to the work ethic; but then he had always been a shining example of the necessity for those with skill not to believe they are exempt from effort. As he has said, playing for England is a slog. Hunt took the view that for all Portugal's record as the leading scorers at this stage, with 14 goals, their defence was vulnerable as the little Koreans had showed. 'Portugal played *open* football . . . and I was looking forward to it.'

Because of Eusebio's four goals when rescuing Portugal in the quarter-final, his team had now become regarded as virtuous, overlooking the indignities they had inflicted on Brazil. Against England, Lucas in midfield and Morais at right-back would both be absent, allegedly with injuries. England made partial provision for dealing with Eusebio by assigning Stiles to mark him man-for-man in the middle of the field, Moore then picking him up when he moved through on the right. Stiles had already proved his capacity to stifle Eusebio in the European Cup, in which Manchester United had beaten Benfica 3-2 at home and 5-1 in Lisbon, the latter match having made George Best's reputation.

Besides Eusebio, Portugal held a threat to any defence in Torres, their six-foot-seven centre-forward; for the first time in the tournament Jack Charlton was going to be given some uncomfortably direct competition in the air. However, if Ramsey was looking for any reassurance, in addition to the opportunities which might be offered by Portugal's defence, it would lie in the fact that of the 14 goals they had scored, six had come from elementary defensive errors: two by Szentmihalyi, two by Manga and two by the Bulgarians, not to mention Korea's five. It was not likely that England would be short of openings, especially as Wembley once again, unusually for July, had a wet, fast top.

It was soon apparent that Portugal's back four of Festa, Baptista, Carlos and Hilario were leaving uncommon gaps and were receiving little reinforcement from Graca and Coluna in midfield, the latter two regarding their prime responsibility as feeding their forwards. Here was a definitive example of a team playing 4-2-4 being at an immediate disadvantage against opposition using three or four men in midfield. Portugal may have helped to make it a marvellous match, but Ball, Bobby Charlton and Peters mostly held a tactical initiative. In the first twenty minutes this resulted in Hurst and Hunt stretching Portugal's defence this way and that, and Pereira's goal remained intact more by luck than judgement.

The menace of Eusebio was being cleverly contained . . . by *not* tackling him. Eusebio usually thrived on judging a tackle about to be made on him, side-stepping it, and bursting clear with his exceptional acceleration. Stiles played it differently. His plan was to get in close but not commit himself, forcing Eusebio to part with the ball. 'It was probably Nobby's best game for England,' Cohen says. 'It was so professional. The idea was to try to keep the ball on Eusebio's left foot, which was the weaker. He was four times faster than Nobby and a foot taller, yet he found for much of the time he couldn't do anything. Nobby was always between him and the goal, was never left trailing, and if he couldn't keep the ball on Eusebio's left side he would force him out wide on the wing.'

The few times that Eusebio did manage to break free of Stiles – who was keeping his physical challenge strictly within the confines of the law and presenting the referee, Schwinte of France, with no need for special vigilance – he found that he was immediately picked up by Moore, on the left of England's defence or, on the right, occasionally by Ball. He became more and more frustrated and depressed, and eventually tactically irresponsible, wanting to take all corner kicks and free-kicks rather than get in to the penalty area where he might create more danger. He was shooting wildly and ineffectually from up to thirty yards, and in the second half Coluna, his captain, and Augusto could be seen shaking their fists at him for what they regarded as tactical timidity. You would never see that from Pelé.

Half an hour had gone when England took the lead: it was a tribute to the quality of the match that the first foul had been committed only eight minutes previously. Now, Wilson sent a long, inward-curving ball ahead of Hunt, who pounded through towards the edge of the penalty area. Already racing out of goal was Pereira, obliged to act as sweeper behind his defence, since neither Festa nor Hilario was giving cover to the centre-backs in their patrol of England's two central strikers. Pereira, attempting to smother the ball at Hunt's feet on the edge of the penalty area with his legs rather than his body, saw it rebound directly to Bobby Charlton, who was closing in behind Hunt in support. Charlton was left with no more difficult a task than to stroke the ball, rather than shoot it, past Pereira and Hunt and into an invitingly open net. It is quite likely that fifteen or twenty years later the goal would not have been allowed: at least according to the most observant member of the England team. 'When Bobby shot, it is almost certain that Roger was in an off-side position slightly beyond the goalkeeper,' Peters says. 'If the linesman had been more harsh, it's my opinion he could have had his flag up.'

However, being behind was neither a new nor frightening experience for the Portuguese, and in what remained of the first half they tested England to the full, and would continue to do so in the second. A drive by Eusebio for once found its way through to Banks so sharply that he could not hold it, but Stiles – who else? – was there to turn it away from danger for a corner. In the second half Coluna began to find gaps with that marvellous left foot, and England's efficiency in defence now posed a fresh problem. Simoes, shackled by Cohen for much of the first half, switched to the right wing, changing places with Augusto, and this served to re-invigorate Portugal's attack. England would need all the defensive graft of Ball, who in this match began to take on a maturity way in advance of his twenty years.

Torres, Augusto and Eusebio might all have levelled the score before England went further ahead with just over ten minutes to go. It was a move of fine English coherence, transferring the ball from one end of the field to the other and into Portugal's net via six men. Jack Charlton, from wide of the penalty area on the left, passed down the line to Ball, who turned the ball inside to Moore. He switched it cross-field to Cohen, advancing over the half-way line. Cohen kept the move in motion with a pass down the right touch-line to Hurst. Nearly losing the ball to Hilario, Hurst won it back and rolled it square into the path of Bobby Charlton, who without checking his stride hit a shot as sweet and stunning as that of Farkas of Hungary against Brazil. Such was the spirit of the match that Charlton was congratulated by Augusto – proving that those who maintain that there is no such thing as good losers, only losers, have got it wrong.

Yet Portugal were not finished. Three minutes later, England conceded their first goal of the tournament as Portugal attacked on full throttle. A high cross from Simoes on the right eluded Banks on the far post. Torres, who had drifted wide, headed back beyond Banks; and Jack Charlton, looking as guilty as a schoolboy pulling his sister's hair, stopped the ball with his hand. Eusebio took the penalty, double-crossed Banks into diving the wrong way and claimed his eighth goal of the tournament. 'It was a strange goal, really,' Banks says. 'I'd come for a cross I couldn't get. Jack left big Torres to wander to the far post, which was unusual for Jack because he was marking him throughout the game. This ball had been whipped over there [by Simoes] and I could see Torres was going to beat anybody, so I tried to go out and get the ball – didn't quite get there, the guy punched it back into the middle where big Jack was standing, and Jack threw out a hand and gave away a penalty. So he gave me a rollicking for missing the cross. I gave him a rollicking for not staying with the big guy. That was because of the disappointment that we were looking as though we were going to concede a goal for the first time in the competition. It was a funny incident, the penalty, because I'd decided which way I was going to dive. Eusebio had scored the majority of his goals in the competition through penalties, and every penalty had gone to the goalkeeper's right and I decided, and I'd said to the lads, 'I am going to dive to my right if there is a penalty.' And here I was confronted by a penalty, everybody facing me and Eusebio walking up to the spot and putting the ball down and all the lads going like this, you see, indicating. And I stood there saying, please, Coluna is looking down the line and seeing all those signs. So Coluna walks up to Eusebio, who's now put the ball down, and they're whispering to each other, so now I'm on the line saying, well, if he knows I'm going to dive to my right he's got to put it to my left. So I dive to my left and he puts it to my right. So I was snookered, you know. I might just have saved it if they hadn't all been giving me the old signal job.'

Now there was a real danger that England might crumble. Simoes was put through by Torres and had Banks at his mercy, only to be foiled yet again by Stiles. A late run by Eusebio carried him through a shaking defence, his pass found Coluna free, and the ball was on its way into the net just under the cross-bar when Banks, his concentration unaffected by the previous goal, made his best and most important save of the finals, somehow managing to turn the ball over the bar.

That was the critical repulse. In the two minutes remaining, Portugal could find nothing more. The whistle went, Jack Charlton sank to his knees, Eusebio was in tears. A 98,000 crowd had had something to savour, best of all that an England team had reached the final. 'This,' said Ramsey, 'was football the way it should be played.' Jack Charlton agreed, even if he had sunk to the ground at the end with relief rather than fatigue. 'It was a great match. I was more anxious than in any other. It had been a breath-taking second goal by Bobby, but Portugal had always troubled us the way they came at us – good technical players. Torres was so strong in the air, I just had to try and make sure he didn't get direct headers at goal, because I couldn't get above him. After their penalty, when there was a few minutes to go, Torres beat me in the air and knocked it square across the box to Eusebio. It looked like 2-2, with Banks not having a chance. But Nobby arrived, he'd read the situation from miles away and just got there in time.'

Moore admitted that they were in difficulty in the closing stages. 'It became scrappy, possibly because we were so near to the final and it made us nervous. We became safety-minded, forgot the basic principles and started to kick anywhere. We lost our rhythm and almost paid for it. Before that, Jack and I had managed Torres okay. We were the right combination – Jack did the basic things, attacking the ball, which he knew he could do, and this gave me more time and space to play. Jack's a strong character. He knows what he wants, what's best for him, and he played that way. He got pleasure out of meeting crosses, but he's not a good passer. "Why don't you knock it away? – if it breaks down in their half there's no trouble for us" was his attitude, yet he wouldn't argue with me doing things that were against his principles.'

Wilson thinks that the score flattered Portugal. 'I think that was the best we played. They hadn't even expected to qualify from their group with Brazil and Hungary. Maybe we bottled it a bit in the last twenty minutes, trying to close it up. It was a bit greasy. I'm not sure panic's the right word, but we helped create our problems. We'd played as well going forward as we would ever do. The Portuguese couldn't play any differently – they *had* to go forward.'

At his official press conference Ramsey was guarded, on account of the warning from FIFA, and said sarcastically that probably every word was being recorded. 'My choice of words on the previous occasion was unfortunate,' he said, 'but it is more unfortunate that I should be subjected to this pressure. But that does not excuse my choice of words.' Of this match he said: 'It was England's greatest victory since I became manager. We have a very good, very efficient side which has done everything that has been asked of them. In the second half we lost our composure, but this was understandable following our punishing match on Saturday.'

Back at the hotel, he told the squad that they could have a drink, but added: 'I mean *one* drink, because we've got a final on Saturday, and then when we've won it, I shall make sure you're permanently drunk.' Or words to that effect. *Tass*, the Soviet news agency, also welcomed a beverage. 'The World Cup semi-final between England and Portugal was like a spring of clear water breaking through the murky sea of dirty football which has covered recent matches in the championships,' it reported. Jean Eskanazi, football sage of *Paris Soir,* was equally encouraged: 'This has been the rehabilitation of football,' he wrote. 'It was everything you want, in football which is not just a street battle.'

9

Jilted Idol

'IT HAUNTS me a bit,' Geoff Hurst has said, 'that it was the start of the slide for Jimmy.' For Jimmy Greaves, the taste for drink in the years following his exclusion from the World Cup Final turned from moderation to excess and thence downwards into uncontrolled compulsion until ultimately, degraded and divorced from his wife, he tried to come to terms with his condition and joined that most compassionate of clubs: Alcoholics Anonymous.

From that trough of helplessness, lurching about in desperation to try to find one more drop at the bottom of one more empty bottle, Jimmy made the most courageous comeback. The extent of his humiliation after he faded from the world of football has been well enough recorded in a television documentary and in his own book, *This One's On Me*, not to need repeating here, and most readers will be familiar with his appearances for ITV Sport and on Channel 4, which have all the old chirpiness of the Cockney sparrow who won a million hearts during the days in which he scored an unbelievable 357 goals in 517 First Division matches for Chelsea, Spurs and West Ham. It was hardly surprising if, the morning that Alf Ramsey told him that he would not be playing in the World Cup Final, momentarily the bottom fell out of his world. No one, not even Jimmy himself, can ever be absolutely sure how much this emotional trauma gnawed at his soul over the next five years and helped to undermine his stability, judgement and self-discipline. Certainly not the slightest responsibility for what subsequently happened can be cast in the direction of Ramsey, whose unenviable decision was regarded as correct in the circumstances by most of the other players: and even, magnanimously, by Greaves himself. Yet it was a shattering experience for one of the greatest players of that or any era, who played with such a spontaneous, instinctive touch, such an unerring eye for goal, that he was rightly regarded as a footballer of genius.

On the field he was contemplated in awe by many of his contemporaries. 'I think he was as good a finisher as I've ever seen in the box,' Armfield says. 'He was two-footed, with amazing balance, and had the killer sense. When he put the ball in the net, he was *smiling*. As a defender, you never knew what he was going to do. When we played down at Tottenham when he made his debut, having just come back from Milan, our trainer said that Jimmy was unlikely to be fit. It didn't stop him scoring three! Jimmy and I went on our first international tour together, and roomed with each other in South America in 1959. He was exceptional.'

In his fifty-seven internationals, only three of them coming after the World Cup in 1966, Greaves scored 44 goals, which leaves him third only to Charlton and Lineker and with a substantially higher average. Moore thought that Ramsey might recall Greaves. He shared a room with him at Hendon Hall, and believed that Greaves himself considered he had a chance right up to the last minute. 'I had thought at first that, if Jim was fit, Alf would bring him back. He would have a far greater psychological effect on the opposition, being recognised world-wide as a great goal-scorer. Yet, on reflection, Alf had no alternative. Geoff scored against Argentina, had a hand in the second goal against Portugal, and we'd played our best football so far. Before the team was announced, Alf called me aside and said, "Your friend's going to be disappointed, I'm not going to bring him back." Yet I had sincerely believed in Jim, one of the all-time greats. You wanted him there. I think he was fit enough, though another whack on his shin would have opened it. But the effect on the opposition would have been enormous. Geoff was just getting started.' Moore disagreed with the hearsay, common at the time, that Greaves was idle. 'Everybody knew what he was like in the penalty area, but what some people didn't appreciate was that it wasn't just speed and skill, it had a lot to do with determination. Men like him and Law and Pelé, they doubled their strength when going in on goal, and you couldn't get them off the ball.'

Others in the team, though sensitive to Greaves's disappointment, are objectively less sympathetic. 'Jimmy wasn't having a great time, he wasn't scoring and he was missing chances,' Jack Charlton says. 'That year, he hadn't made the position his own, partly because of his jaundice. I suspect Alf had wanted to bring in Geoff for some time, but his loyalty was such he'd found it difficult to leave Greaves out.' Bobby Charlton is even more detached on the issue. 'I felt sorry for all our reserves. We were a squad, and Alf had nurtured it. At the final whistle against Germany, when Ron Flowers and Gerry Byrne came out on the pitch, I felt very much for those who hadn't played. But I never gave the matter over Jimmy much thought, it was blown up out of proportion, and I was confident Alf would do the right thing. Hurst was better suited to the competition as it was. He was the target man up front. Hurst was good in the air, more suited to England's needs. I don't think Greaves's reputation meant so much to Alf – that was part of Alf's quality.'

At the time of his retirement from Manchester United in 1973, Charlton had written: 'Jimmy was a bit of a luxury, I always felt. He'd score five if you won 8-0, but in matches where a single goal would decide, it was better to have someone like Hurst. You never saw Jimmy much in a game, he was waiting up there to score, and I suppose that's why he never really materialised for Alf. I've cursed Jimmy at times, he scored such fantastic goals against us in the league or cup for Spurs, but playing for England is different, it is a slog. You couldn't rely on him to score the only goal, and then hang on to it. Roger Hunt was always criticised. He seemed the odd man out to the public, but he was very unselfish, he never complained at the running he did.' There is truth in Charlton's observations on Greaves, but it should also be said that he himself stood to profit more from the company of Hurst or Hunt.

Any idea, however, that Bobby Charlton was either uncaring or selfish is dispelled by John Connelly. 'If you were having a bad time, Bob would always come and have a word in your ear. He was one of the first to invite Jimmy to come and play in charity fixtures, to bring him back in when he was recovering [with AA]. Bobby was very good that way. People sometimes thought he was aloof, but he was just shy and retiring. Quite honestly, most of us thought there'd be no change for the final, but Roger *did* think so. He'd personally had a good World Cup, scored goals, worked hard, was popular in the squad. Yet *he* doubted himself. The London press was plugging for Greaves, of course, and I remember thinking, when the team was announced, that he wouldn't put a boot on again for England. He was sick. It was the most disappointing thing of his life. It was the same for me, when I was left out.'

For a few days after the injury against France, Greaves had had to keep his leg out of water when taking a bath, but once the stitches had been removed, his condition improved and after the semi-final against Portugal he was certainly fit. I remember watching him in a training spell in the morning, out at London Colney, and there was no doubt about his sharpness, as the crescendo of public controversy reached its peak in the press and on television. 'It was one of those fateful things,' Wilson reflected. Greaves was playing a game of poker with nothing in his hand.

Cohen thinks that Ramsey may even have been allowing the injury to act as a kind of camouflage of his intentions, out of kindness to Greaves. 'Hurst hadn't yet convinced everyone, had he, and Jimmy looked terrible when he was told – his face was as long as a Greenline bus. But can you blame him? Out of a World Cup Final, at home. Hunt, now *there* was a player you needed around in an international team. He would take the stick for Greaves, take the knocks when the boots were flying in the box. He was a players' player. Even if you gave him a bad pass he would make you look good by his willingness to run. You could count on him if you were in a corner and looking up field for somewhere to stick the ball. When you played against Liverpool, Roger was always on the end of everything, always there underneath the high ones. A terrific guy.'

The rest of the team, aware of Ramsey's dilemma and Greaves's anguish, were nevertheless a squad in action, and with that thirst for success without which nothing could be achieved. One man's sorrow could not be allowed to obstruct the objective. 'I was too young, too involved in myself to remember,' Ball says. 'The controversy didn't register, I was just delighted to be playing. With Geoff, I could always bounce the ball off him, build something. He would help to get you into the team. With Jimmy, you had to play for *him*. Geoff could do more for our team. With Roger, you had to hit him into channels, because he hadn't got the same touch, but with Jimmy you couldn't build off the front two. Jimmy was sniffing, Roger was running. So with Geoff there, you still had two goal-scorers but you got more from the team. I think that disappointment helped to put Jimmy off the rails, though only he could say it. He'd set his heart on that World Cup, and Geoff was his deputy.'

It was apparent to those close to the squad that, by the end of the tour following Lilleshall, Hunt, formerly an alternative to Greaves, had now become one of Ramsey's pillars because of his consistency. After the match in Norway, Ramsey had said contentedly: 'Roger *always* plays well.' Yet that was not the view of a nation winding itself up with expectation back home. Because of his size, and an appearance of heaviness, because he occasionally fluffed simple chances close in when he had to turn quickly, Hunt was regarded as an impediment by many casual observers, and especially by the London press. This attitude was reflected in one of the humorous columns which at that time Michael Parkinson was writing for the *Sunday Times*. In the middle of the World Cup, on behalf of the 'Greaves Club,' Parkinson gently satirised the 'Hunt school':

'Well, of course Roger's always *there*, as we say in the business. Always taking the weight off the other players, always challenging. Now with these modern defensive tactics you've got two chances of getting through. One is on the outside of the full-back, and the sharp cross into the middle. Centering, I think they used to call it. It was at one time, I believe, done by people called wingers. Well, that's one way. The other is the old one-two through the centre: laying it off, making space, getting possession, and beating the goalkeeper. Scoring, I think, is the old term. Now this is where Roger is so good. He's always making space.'

'Roger *who*?'

Hunt stoically rode the insults. He was used to uncertainty. In four years prior to the World Cup, he had gained only thirteen caps, had been on three summer tours and only played twice; he went without a game with Winterbottom in the 1962 World Cup, made one appearance against East Germany in 1963 when Greaves was ill, another in 1964 against Portugal. Yet, for Liverpool, he was a model scorer, with 245 goals by the time he retired, and enjoyed a faithful audience which would fill Anfield for his testimonial.

'I used to get that much stick from the Wembley crowd,' he recalls. 'I was really an old-fashioned inside-forward, used to playing with wingers. Then the game started changing, with two central strikers and still two wingers. When we started playing 4-4-2, without wingers, I was under more pressure: more running, more effort to make space for others. I couldn't show what I could do at club level. I found it more difficult, the role, the system, than with the club. It would have been more difficult anyway, because of the quality, but I didn't see a lot of the ball. The Wembley crowd weren't very kind to me. There was this thing, with Jimmy playing for Tottenham, and I was the northerner who took his place, so I was never popular. I was aware of that.

'Playing with Alf did give me valuable experience, playing with and against great players, in famous stadiums, in important games, so that I went back home feeling confident. But it was a completely different role there, when I could come back more, or get behind the full-back. My goal-scoring record with England was better between 1962 and 1964 than later. On tour in 1966, I played in three matches, Jimmy in two. Yet throughout the first three World Cup games, I felt under pressure for my place. Then, with Jimmy on the side-lines, and such a goal-scorer, both Geoff and I must have felt the same. We wouldn't have been surprised if he'd been recalled. Alf went for reliable people, but you couldn't be sure in that situation. I wasn't a regular before the World Cup, and didn't feel a regular till it was all over. I never really knew Alf. He was separate from the players. I did like him, because he was loyal, he put the players before everyone else.

'Before the World Cup, when he announced the shirt numbers, they seemed to be what he thought the team would be. Ball was No. 7, Greaves eight, Bobby Charlton nine, myself ten and Connelly eleven. I'd had the best run, up to Hampden before the tour, I'd ever had. But so much of the time it had been Jimmy or me. Of the six times I was dropped, five times it was for Jimmy, and I was the first to be dropped after the World Cup, against Scotland the following year, and again was replaced by Jimmy. I didn't play particularly well against France in the third match. We were never in trouble, but it was not spectacular. Yet after three games I'd scored three goals, and my confidence was improving. On the Friday night, after the semi-final, we were going to the cinema, and as we got off the coach Alf took me aside and said I was playing in the final. That wasn't his normal style, usually the team was announced on the coach after training. That was the only time that happened to me. He didn't ask me not to tell anyone, but I didn't. I had an inkling it was a confidence.'

Ramsey recognised what other members of the team also saw. 'He wasn't just a fine goal-scorer, his judgement on passing was so accurate that he helped you know what you could achieve,' Ian Callaghan says. Jack Charlton, himself to become an astute manager, agrees: 'Roger was not a good header, but he was a great runner. He was the forgotten man of the team. What he did, one of the main assets of a forward, was that he moved *before* the ball, shifting defenders about. He was marvellous at this, he gave colleagues an option. When you're a centre-back, they're the kind you hate to play against, you're always thinking, "Why don't you stand still?" You've got to adjust your position all the time. When a forward stands still, you can get a breather.'

An irony of the situation was that, at half-time during the opening match against Uruguay, Greaves had been among those who discussed with Ramsey the possibility of pushing forward someone to stand with their sweeper, Troche, and nullify his freedom. 'Somebody who could lay it off quickly, because that would have helped,' Greaves remembers. Inadvertently, he was plotting his own demise.

The glory of the victory in 1966 brought mixed emotion for Hunt, and would affect his career, too. After public criticism of his performance against Rumania in 1969, he asked Ramsey to leave him out of the next match. 'Nobody likes to be criticised. You accept it as a professional, it's part of the job. But I had had a lot. *I* was the one who replaced Greaves. I didn't want to be the one up front at the age of 32, with all the load and the responsibility of carrying the burden *again.* Not physically, but mentally. I didn't want another World Cup.'

At the time, my opinion was that if Ramsey was to make a change for the final – which was against every established concept of keeping to a winning team, never mind the tactics – it would be to recall Greaves for Hurst, though I thought it unlikely. We did not, at that time, know that much about Hurst, while Hunt had become an established figure of Ramsey's. History would prove, as Hunt's instinct told him, that he was the more expendable. Hurst, a bit like Ball, was in a state of euphoria *before* the final. He said to commentator Martin Tyler: 'After Argentina and Portugal, the rest was up to others. I came to the final satisfied, like after a win at the races – you're now betting with the bookies' money. It would have made the Greaves thing even more horrible if I had taken his place and had a total stunner . . . you have to remember not too many people agreed with Alf on the morning of the match. I had to astonish half of Britain that afternoon, just to stop them wanting to string Alf up for leaving Jimmy on the bench.'

Hurst, like Hunt, was told the night before the final that he was playing. Greaves was not told that he was not, and it made the anguish the more intense. He says that he was aware of Moore's opinion that he might be recalled, talking it over in their room, but did not agree, and he knew that Moore had no inside information on Ramsey's planning. Moore had no knowledge on the Friday night that Greaves was out.

'But *I* knew,' Greaves says. 'One day on the coach, I think it was Thursday, I was sitting next to Harold Shepherdson on the way back from training, and I said casually, "I suppose it's going to be difficult to get back," and he turned away and looked out of the window. I was close to Harold, he'd been there ever since I came into the squad. Alf had obviously confided in him, and he was too embarrassed to answer me. The final was a big, jubilant thing. I'd played the first three matches, and when I was told I was out I was choked, but there was no one to blame. In the cold light of day, Alf made all the right decisions. He seems even more right now than he did then. People drummed up the Ramsey-Greaves clash, but there wasn't one. I never fell out with him, or had a bad word with or about him. It was a great blow, because I'd always known in my heart we were going to win, and I'd thought I'd be in, without being big-headed. Nobody sent me up more than *I* did about me being a lazy bastard, but I'd fought hard to get back after my hepatitis. It was the greatest disappointment of my life . . . and I hope it always will be! I don't want another.

'There was a lot of division about me and Roger – the cult hero, as it were, and the anti-hero. But I'd have done the same as Alf.

86

The only thing I might have done differently was tell me earlier. That would have saved me the days of grasping at straws that I might be there. I could have lived these days easier. But maybe he had his reason, not to let the opposition know. I could have kept it private, but maybe he didn't think he could. I guess I could have handled it.

'It's said it depressed me in subsequent seasons. Not really. I had a great season in 1966-67, my last good season. I scored 38 goals' – imagine that *today* – 'and we won the cup at Tottenham, and I played twice for England. My split with Alf wasn't really a split. In 1967, England were due to go to Canada with a depleted squad, and I said to him privately, "Honest, Alf, what's the point? It's over, I don't want to turn up if I'm not going to be in the team." From that moment on Alf accepted that I was no longer in line.

'The booze didn't develop out of the World Cup, it came more out of my move to West Ham. I left Tottenham in '69, and it was all downhill from then on. West Ham were a bad side when I got there. I was in an exchange with Peters. Hurst had lost a bit of his enthusiasm. There was some question of Moore going, and the atmosphere was bad. Peters had seen the signs: Ron had lost it, and was going through a bad stage of his career. Maybe Chelsea was the best part of my playing days, but I enjoyed Spurs until the last few months. I wasn't on the way to being an alcoholic then. I was drinking heavily, but there were other drinkers at Tottenham, such as Dave Mackay and Alan Gilzean. My mistake was to accept Bill Nicholson's suggestion that I should go to West Ham in exchange for Peters. I should have told him that if he wanted him, he should go and buy him. The trouble was that there were rumours about me becoming a rally driver, and Bill thought I was going to jack it in. Of course I wasn't. If I'd stayed, perhaps I'd have got over the blues with Tottenham. But the drink? There was no alternative to that. It was probably inevitable, but I don't know why.'

We can never measure our own or others' personalities, or be certain what motivates one or restricts another. 'There's got to be a lot of self-discipline to get over alcoholism,' Cohen says, 'and if Jimmy had had more of it before, he might have been an even better player. Johnny Haynes used to put away plenty of large vodkas, but he'd train his backside off the next day. Yet in Alan Mullery's book, he recounts that Greaves asked at Tottenham to be left out against Chelsea because "Chopper Harris never gives me a kick".' That indeed reflects Greaves's nature: happy go lucky one moment, distraught deep inside when omitted by Ramsey. 'He was,' Armfield says, 'a very sensitive boy.'

Greaves tried hard to keep up a face. He went round the dressing-room before the kick-off wishing everyone the best of luck, still smiling, still the same old Jim, it seemed, even if inside his heart was broken. When, as the triumphant forces finally left the pitch after the celebrations with the Cup, and the band kept up the strains of 'When the Saints Go Marching In' – a cruel echo of happy times at Tottenham – there was Jack Charlton, the old man of the game, walking off with his arm round Greaves. It had been a genuine team. 'He'd been a part, and now he wasn't,' Jack reflects. In the morning, Bobby Moore had asked Greaves why he was packing his bags: was he not going to be there for the celebration when they won? Greaves didn't answer. At the official dinner in the evening at the Royal Garden Hotel, Ramsey came up to Moore and asked, 'Where's your friend?' Moore assured him that there was no animosity or bitterness. 'It's just he'd rather be away from it all.'

10

Winning the Cup Twice

ONE OF THE rituals of Ramsey's squad was an evening visit to the cinema, usually to some cowboy film for which the manager had a penchant; and though there would often be derisive jeers of 'We've already seen that once', Harold Shepherdson would be dispatched to the telephone to book twenty-five seats. So it was off to the flicks again the night before the final, though nobody can tell you what the film was. The only memory is for those who were told on the way they would be playing. They went early to bed afterwards, but few of them would sleep for long. Stiles was awake before seven, rose without waking Ball, and went to church, being a Catholic. He returned to bed afterwards and still did not sleep, having been awake almost the whole night. The visit to church was not particularly religious, though he did try to go most Sundays. 'If you want something, you go to church to ask for it. You don't always get it.' Well before breakfast, the ground floor of the hotel was littered with cables and television personnel, the police closing the gates to keep out the hundreds of fans who began to gather.

When a kick-off is in the afternoon the worst hours of the day are between breakfast and lunch, a yawning gap in which the minutes seem like hours. To fill it, some of the players went shopping. Bobby Charlton and Wilson bought shirts. Jack Charlton remembers Ball spending £300 on a watch. Others just wandered about in Golders Green, having a quiet coffee, often unrecognised. To travel to and from the hotel they just hopped on a bus: a far cry from the security hassle of today. Down at FIFA's headquarters in the West End there had been wrangling over whether Beckenbauer had received a second booking in the semi-final. The Germans claimed it was a case of mistaken identity for

Overath by the referee. The disciplinary committee accepted the appeal: they could hardly do otherwise, having allowed Garrincha to play in the 1962 final after he had previously been sent off. With England never having lost to West Germany, and having beaten them home and away in the past twelve months, 13 to 8 on England was the bookmakers' offer.

Reading the morning papers, England's players saw a warning from George Raynor, the English manager of Sweden in the 1958 final, who said that the home side must be ready for the goal-scoring potential of Beckenbauer in addition to the five scoring specialists in front of him. 'He plays the wall-pass better than anyone I've seen. I can't see any answer to him.' Ramsey was to prove he *had* the answer. Helmut Schoen had more to worry about, meanwhile, than pleading with FIFA for Beckenbauer's availability. Höttges, his right-back from Bremen, who had missed the semi-final with an injury, was now reckoned to be fit, and would be detailed to shadow Hurst in Germany's man-for-man system operating in front of Schulz, the sweeper. Would Höttges's ankle stand up to it? Schoen hoped it would, and took the gamble. 'Horst was not technically refined, but he was a fighter – not dirty, a fighter who was clean,' Schoen said. In his sixteen years in charge, Schoen did not make many misjudgements, and this was hardly one of them, for Höttges, who had played throughout the previous year, was one of his most dependable players. Schoen himself had come from the engine-room, which breeds understanding: a tall inside-forward, who had scored seventeen times in sixteen appearances, limited by the start of the Second World War. Aged sixteen, an amateur with Dresden Sports Club, he had been coached by Jimmy Hogan from England, who had handed him over to Waldemar Gerschler, the trainer of the 800 metres world record holder, Rudolf Harbig. 'Make him a player, physically,' Hogan had asked. Schoen had been manager of Saaland, in the 1953-54 qualifying competition, before they amalgamated with West Germany and he became Herberger's assistant.

Schoen also had a problem with his goalkeeper, Tilkowski, who had taken one or two knocks and had been the original third choice. The manager had confidence in him. 'He was not a showman, he was practical, quiet, and solid like Banks.' Schoen's only other selection decision was whether to persist with Emmerich, who had little impact against Russia. 'Yet we knew that Cohen liked to attack,' Schoen said, 'so we hoped to exploit Emmerich. We felt the rest of the team was strong enough to take that chance.'

The strength lay in trusted performers such as Schulz, Weber and Schnellinger in defence, Haller and Overath in midfield,

Seeler and Held in attack. 'Seeler was an ideal captain, he never gave in,' Schoen says. 'He could carry the team with him. I could always take a risk with him if he had a slight injury, because of the value of his personality. Schulz, at the back, was not a great player but had a sound tactical sense. He was reliable, a good organiser from Herberger's time, and I wouldn't have wanted to play against him. I'd known Schnellinger since he was in the youth team with me, he'd played midfield in the 1958 World Cup and had a lot of experience in Italy. Weber was similar to Schulz, but more of a player and very athletic. Haller, from Milan, was a great technician, though not a fighter. He was an old-fashioned inside-right, and when he had the ball something could always happen. He was not strong in defence, but he pleased other players. Held, from Dortmund, was fast but not a match-maker. I could not be sure what he would do, but nor could the opposition.'

And, of course, there was Beckenbauer. The rival managers, sadly for the public, independently gave the same cautious role to their respective star players: they would shadow each other. Bobby Charlton, the perfect professional, was prepared to sacrifice himself in his country's interest: an attitude that was applicable to England's most famous cricketer of the Eighties. 'We reckoned we would win unless we did something stupid,' Bobby says. 'We were only concerned about one or two of them – Beckenbauer, and maybe Overath and Seeler, although I thought Seeler lost something by his responsibility as captain. Playing in Italy had made Schnellinger and Haller more elegant, but they tended to be prima donnas. Overath had range with his passing to change direction, but what he didn't have, and Beckenbauer did, was pace. Beckenbauer was the find . . . the new young player with the imagination and the daring to attack defenders and to get into danger areas. So we had to make sure we did the right thing against those two. Seeler was small but he was bloody brave, and he would go in for anything. He climbed heights that people his size really shouldn't try, and he could crack the ball. There was Emmerich, the left-winger, who was dangerous because he was unorthodox. We weren't frightened of him, but he hit the ball from daft angles. After the semi-finals, everybody suddenly said that I was the one they'd got to watch. I think it detracted from Beckenbauer's skill, shadowing me, and I was quite pleased to see that he was there with me. Alf had said to me, "Whatever happens, I don't expect you to be going in one direction and him to be going in another." I used to have pretty good legs and I was a good runner, ninety minutes was no problem to me. I knew it would not release me to enjoy the game as much as I would have liked, but I was prepared to do it if we were going to win. I must admit I was quite surprised that he was marking me as well, and we near enough cancelled each other out . . . but at the end of the day the one who's justified in the decision is the one that wins, and I think we did well by it and I felt sorry for Franz.'

The scene in the dressing-room little more than half an hour before the start was chaotic, the place buzzing with people incidental to the action. Moore remarked to Jack Charlton that it didn't seem much like the number one cup final in football, but Jack said, 'That's why it's like this.' Peters sat quietly thinking about Overath, his opposite number in Germany's midfield, against whom, since 1959, he had played at Youth, Under 23 and senior level, knowing now just how good a player he was. Stiles, like several of the others, was meticulously following personal superstitions. He had been out to look at the pitch before playing Uruguay: such was the performance that thereafter he had stayed in the dressing-room. Now, by turn, he was putting his shorts on first, placing his feet in a bath before putting on his socks, soft-soaping his boots, putting them on, oiling his legs having taken his shorts off again, washing his hands, back on with the shorts, contact lenses in, teeth out, vaseline over the eyes to stop the perspiration trickling in. 'I was ready! It took me an hour. Everybody has different habits, you know. What I remember was the FA Committee coming in and wishing us all the best, and Ray Wilson, I don't know if Ray remembers this, but he's walking along and one of the Committee – I won't say which one, he's dead now – he came up and said to Ray, "All the best, George," and I was killing myself laughing. He'd remembered my name, but Ray had been playing for England for years and I thought, how could he do that? . . . mistake him for George Cohen . . .'

Ball could not wait to get out on the pitch. He had been telling Stiles half the night how he was going to destroy Schnellinger, which says something for the confidence of one of the least experienced players facing the most experienced. 'Nobby and I roomed together and I think there wasn't an ounce of fear in our bodies,' Ball says. 'The words of my father kept coming back to me in the dressing-room. I kept looking round at other people and some were very nervous. Alf was going round . . . all the last minute things you've got to remember, free-kicks, corners and so on. I was too young to have nerves. It was the most instinctive game I've ever played. I didn't play to any orders. I just worked and ran. And enjoyed it. I've always said about Wembley that you're either terrified when you walk out there or you absolutely love it, and, thank God for me, I walked out and the roar just exploded in your ears and I took a deep breath and said, I love this, this is for me. I remember letting my Dad know I was picked and he'd said, "You lucky little devil, this has got to be the greatest day of your life. Live every minute of it, take everything in, because it will be over in a flash, but you'll be good enough out there today.'''

It had been raining on and off for the past forty-eight hours, and as Banks looked up the tunnel, he knew he'd have to put his gloves on. 'It was going to be difficult for the goalkeeper, because the ball at Wembley comes off very quick when it's wet, and so I had to make sure that the studs were right. The keeper has to make sure he's got a good grip underneath, and also that he has an extra pair of gloves in case the others get very wet. It was a bit disconcerting, as all the other games had been played when I didn't need gloves.' Cohen remembers the muted noise of the crowd inside the tunnel, then blasting his mind as they came out on the pitch . . . and not much else, until they were into the game. These were the teams that lined up to shake hands with the Queen on 30 July:

ENGLAND
(1-4-1-3-2)

Gordon Banks
(Leicester)

George Cohen   Jack Charlton   Bobby Moore   Ray Wilson
(Fulham)   (Leeds)   (West Ham)   (Everton)

Nobby Stiles
(Manchester United)

Alan Ball   Bobby Charlton   Martin Peters
(Blackpool)   (Manchester United)   (West Ham)

Geoff Hurst   Roger Hunt
(West Ham)   (Liverpool)

★

Lothar Emmerich   Sigi Held   Uwe Seeler
(Borussia, Dortmund) (Borussia, Dortmund)   (Hamburg)
Wolfgang Overath   Franz Beckenbauer   Helmut Haller
(Cologne)   (Bayern, Munich)   (Bologna)
Karl-Heinz Schneillinger   Wolfgang Weber   Horst Höttges
(AC Milan)   (Cologne)   (Werder, Bremen)
                       Willi Schulz
                       (Hamburg)
                    Hans Tilkowski
               (Borussia, Dortmund)

WEST GERMANY
(1-1-3-3-3)

Referee: Gottfried Dienst (Switzerland)

It used to be said, good-naturedly, that Cohen's crosses were more dangerous to the crowd behind the goal than they were to the opposition; to which he would answer that he got in more crosses than most wingers. The first minute of the match gave an indication of this, and of the kind of open, appealing spectacle which was to follow: end to end play, as the old-time scribes dutifully used to write. Put free by Bobby Charlton's square pass, Cohen drove a firm ball to the far post where Hurst, air-borne and on cue, headed down strongly, and Tilkowski had to scramble the ball away from inside the foot of the post. The Germans had had their first feel of Hurst.

Seeler, with that heavy gait which belied his agility, made ground at the other end to test Banks with a 25-yard shot, which was tipped clear. The shells were already falling. A long clearance by Schulz was fed by Emmerich on to Held, who pulled his shot wide. Jack Charlton, advancing into Germany's half, found Peters on the left. Cutting in, Peters let fly, and his cross shot was turned round the right-hand post by a diving Tilkowski: four shots in as many minutes.

If Germany had a persistent fault, it was their propensity for making a meal of any foul inflicted upon them, harsh or not, and soon Weber was lectured by Dienst for staying down after a minor challenge. Bobby Charlton, moving left to draw Beckenbauer, whose continuous presence would have done credit to an industrious sheep-dog, sent Ball through the middle, and a pass to the right found Peters, who was constantly searching for, and finding, spaces: but he shot tamely. With only eight minutes gone, the crowd had already been roused more times than in the entire match against Uruguay. Hurst, coming deep to try to lose Höttges, slipped a ball to Stiles, whose cross was headed out by Höttges straight to Bobby Charlton, his blind side run for once having stranded Beckenbauer. Charlton lofted the ball back first time, and Hurst, now coming in from deep, had the ball punched off his eyebrows by Tilkowski. West Germany's was the more threatened goal, but now they took the lead from the first unforced error England had made in the finals. A ripple of passes across the middle of the field, Haller-Seeler-Schnellinger, took the ball to Held on the left flank. He lofted a high cross, which was falling harmlessly towards Wilson, clear of the six-yard area. 'It was going beyond Ray and out for a goal-kick, and I shouted leave it,' Banks says. 'But Ray wasn't too sure about Haller and decided he'd better not take a chance in case Haller tried to come round the back of him, so he headed it, but the ball dropped straight at Haller's feet. He only half hit the shot, but Jack had come in to cover, and was standing about three feet away. The ball was travelling between us, and Jack went as though he was going to try to stop it. I couldn't move until it had come past in case there was a deflection, and by the time I went down it was on top of me and I was too late, and it skidded into the corner. Jack and I just looked at each other as much as to say, come on, let's get back into it.' For the first time, England were behind.

Wilson is still kicking himself long afterwards. 'It was an awful mistake, no doubt about that, it was a third division ball,' he says. 'I had a lot of time, and I doubted if Haller would come in and challenge me for it, but then I had an awful feeling that Seeler might be lurking somewhere behind. With the indecision, I was rocking on my heels, and I finished up with this marsh-mallow header. It just dropped down for the lad, and bingo – knock it in. It was the only time I was grateful to be 31. If I'd been younger it could have destroyed my game. I looked at Jack. It wasn't just unlike me, it was unlike anyone in the defence over the last few years. Alf said afterwards, "That's the first mistake you've made for me in four years." I sit back sometimes and think about it, the sort of mistakes like that which cost matches, Moore's in Poland and Hunter's at Wembley in 1973.' Now, he just got on with the game.

Schoen thought to himself on the bench, 'It's not the end of the match by a long way.' Within six minutes, England confirmed this. Moore, making ground on the left, swivelled out of a challenge by Overath and had his heel taken. He fell with one hand on the ball, enabling him to place it instantly for the free-kick. A quick three paces back, and he saw Hurst preparing for a diagonal run from the right. With a telepathy bred by months of practice and play with West Ham, Moore dipped the kick in towards the left post, and sure enough there was Hurst's head on the end of it, hammering the ball down into the corner of the net beyond Tilkowski, with the defence caught square across the box.

The Germans could argue that Overath had been prevented from getting back into defence at the moment of Moore's kick because Dienst was still lecturing him about the foul, which had been innocent enough. The next moment Dienst was to show an inconsistency when he ordered another free-kick to be retaken. Such is the rub of the green. From this point of recovery, it looked as if England would now gallop away with the match, for between then and half-time the proportion of chances or half-chances fell five to one in their favour. Ball was beginning to stretch the opposition, getting and giving the ball in an endless buzz of enthusiasm. From a run down the left, he turned the ball back into the path of Bobby Charlton twenty yards out, but as Charlton swung his foot, there, already blocking the route to goal, was the inevitable Beckenbauer. The pair of them moved about the pitch side by side like partners in an ice-dance. Beckenbauer was equally restricted by the duet, and when he did get forward once to combine with Seeler and make an opening for Haller, a dash by Banks off his line snuffed the chance before Haller could think.

Yet the play was in a contradictory state: England had control, but not the advantage. Whenever Hunt or Hurst seemed likely to evade Weber or Höttges, there was Schulz prowling back and forth to stifle further advance, forcing England to move wide and away from danger. However, Emmerich had given the orchestra of German claxons nothing to celebrate, Cohen tightly subduing him. When, around the half-hour, Jack Charlton conceded a corner, following which Banks punched out a shot by Overath, Emmerich's immediate answering volley was without menace, held by Banks with one eye on where he was going to prompt England's next attack. The somnolence of Emmerich was giving Cohen scope to attack, and from a long cross to the far post Hurst headed down, Tilkowski reached the ball but lost it, and Ball was there to snap up possession on the bye-line close to the post. Dribbling away from goal, he suddenly turned and stabbed the ball square towards the penalty spot, but Overath was back to hook clear.

Six minutes before half-time a blast from Overath was too powerful for Banks to hold, and the parried ball ran clear to Emmerich. Again his return shot lacked sting. At the other end Hunt, winning a heading duel, shot from an acute angle and Tilkowski was able easily to cover. Bobby Charlton, weaving this way and that, turned away from the sentry-like figure of Beckenbauer and threaded a pass through to Peters on the edge of the area, but he was blocked. The last arrow of the first half was Germany's. A reverse pass on the half-way line from Held sent Seeler clear: with the defence retreating ahead of him, he suddenly shot from 25 yards and Banks had to make one of his best saves.

Back in the dressing-room, there was disagreement between Hunt and his manager over the time and space being given to Schulz to operate his security screen behind the back four. With substantially more of the game, England had nothing to show for it. 'Alf had wanted Geoff and me to push up as far as possible, he didn't want the sweeper to be comfortable,' Hunt says. 'Well, for the first quarter of an hour I didn't get a kick, so I started to come a little bit deeper to get hold of the ball a bit, which meant I was bringing my marker away from the sweeper, which wasn't what Alf wanted, and he was going on at me about it.' Ramsey, though, could be satisfied that the ploy of putting Charlton on Beckenbauer had reduced Germany's midfield effectiveness by preventing Beckenbauer playing his one-twos with Seeler to open up the field.

*Greaves dazzles Mexico, but the goal touch
is missing.*

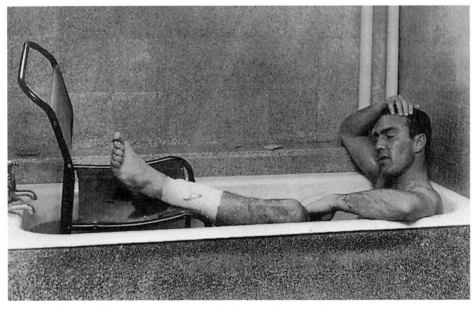

*Soaking up the nervous strain of nursing a
cut shin after the match against France.
The gash was to cost him his place.*

Semi-final duel. Wherever Eusbeio (left) might go, Stiles (right) was usually there to frustrate him. Eusbeio's colleagues criticised his lack of tactical intelligence and persistence.

Another Bobby flier! Charlton's second goal against Portugal, as memorable as that against Mexico, establishes a two-goal lead.

Hunt jumps over the Portugal goalkeeper Pereira and the ball rebounds to Bobby Charlton (out of picture), who scores England's first goal. Was Hunt off-side?

2-2: Weber (on ground, left) scoops the ball past Wilson and Banks. Moore appeals for hand-ball by Schnellinger, Cohen is on his knees. Peters, Seeler, Schnellinger and Jack Charlton freeze.

Portugal worried England's defence in the last 20 minutes, reducing the lead with a penalty, and might have equalised but for the dependability of Banks in goal, seen here frustrating Augusto.

3-2: Hurst (out of picture) has hit the underside of the cross-bar, Tilkowski twists to see the ball bouncing up from the line, Hunt, in front of Weber, is about to appeal for a goal.

4-2: Pow! The first hat-trick in a World Cup Final. Beckenbauer can only watch, exhausted.

We did it! Left to right: Banks, Ball, Hunt, Hurst, Moore, Wilson, Cohen, Bobby Charlton.

Moore offers the Cup to his manager, while the toothless Stiles and others try in vain to drag a reluctant Ramsey with them on a lap of honour.

The start of the second half was accompanied by rain slanting through the sun-rays, and there was the encouraging sight of Ball beginning to torment Schnellinger. Once, his acceleration created space for Bobby Charlton, but, stumbling clear of Beckenbauer's tackle he was pinned by another. Ten minutes into the half Germany seemed static and short of ideas. Seeler was chopped down by Moore, who then gently helped him back to his feet. Moore's studious distribution from the back was a prime source of English initiative: it was from him that Hunt and Peters continued a move which ended with Bobby Charlton's high cross being punched clear by Tilkowski. The crowd, denied a goal, made up for it by mildly denigrating the referee with that venerated hymn 'Oh, oh, what a referee', little knowing how grateful they would later have cause to be. Although Held was now beginning to cause trouble down England's right flank, the game continued to flow mostly towards Tilkowski. Jack Charlton headed wide from Moore's free-kick, and from another arching header by Hurst, this time down to the feet of Bobby Charlton, a goal seemed certain. Somehow Beckenbauer managed to get in the way, colliding with Tilkowski, who was struck by the ball which cannoned clear. Tilkowski took several moments to recover, and he was still in something of a daze minutes later when Peters crossed from the left, a defensive header glanced the ball away to the right, and Bobby Charlton, his right foot a blur, hammered a shot across the face of the goal and back past the left post.

England were pressing hard now, and their flexibility was emphasised when, with nine men retreating behind a counter-thrust, it was Ball who won the critical tackle on the edge of the English penalty area. The next moment it was the same boy-faced player, legs pumping like pistons, who was dashing in to force a save out of Tilkowski. No goalkeeper, except perhaps the North Korean in the quarter-final, had been so busy in the previous 31 matches. A goal was due: and arrived in the 78th minute.

A ball from the right was deflected to Hurst on the left of Germany's penalty area. He turned left and right tightly, to work some space clear of the two defenders hemming him in, got sight of goal and let fly. The shot was deflected and deadened by Höttges, and while several hesitated, Peters stole in to drive past Tilkowski. 'It was a corner from Ball, which was headed out to Hurst,' Peters says, 'and he probably shouldn't have shot because the angle was too tight. Höttges stuck out a leg and the ball went up in front of me, and I only thought of keeping it down, I didn't really try to place it, and the keeper went one way and Schnellinger, I think, the other, and the ball went straight down the middle.' The fortune for England, in all probability, was that the ball had not fallen for Jack Charlton: at least, that is his version.

'I was running in at the far post,' he says, 'when the ball struck somebody and looped up towards me, and I was on my own it seemed to me, it was going to drop perfect for me, and I remember thinking to myself, "Oh hell, it really is coming to me" – and the goal looked that big and I was only about five yards out, and while I'm thinking . . . suddenly Martin pops up in front of me and knocks it in, and I went "Great, terrific", you know. I was delighted.' It speaks of the difference between defender and attacker that while Charlton was still thinking, Peters was already moving; and, more remarkable, that Peters says he had time to look along the line and make sure that he was not off-side. Ahead of his time, indeed.

Now the Germans had little to offer as the remaining minutes slipped by, and England's reserves, having come down from their seats in the stand, were grouped behind the England bench, awaiting the moment of victory. Ball left Schnellinger in a heap of legs as he cut inside, but his pass to Hurst was squandered as Hurst snatchily drove wide. Never a team to give in, the Germans were none the less hard pressed to prevent the margin being increased. Höttges felled the flying Ball from behind. Hurst, off-side, wasted time by lobbing over the cross-bar and Jack Charlton elicited a howl of German whistles from the terraces with a back pass as long as a station platform. 'Rule Britannia' sang the home supporters: and Stiles promptly chopped down Held.

With five minutes left, Weber glanced wide a free-kick by Emmerich. The Germans were throwing defenders forward all they dared. Beckenbauer, bouncing two wall-passes off colleagues, forced a corner, but was eighty yards distant moments later to smother Bobby Charlton: a run of Herculean discipline. There was just over a minute remaining when Overath, the Germans now taking any risk, lashed a shot across the six-yard area. How the claxons hooted, and their reward was at hand.

Moving forward to challenge for a ball in the air on the right-hand edge of the penalty area, Jack Charlton had his eyes on the target as he jumped above Held, who made no attempt to meet the ball but stooped, making a back for Charlton. Extraordinarily, Dienst gave a free-kick against Charlton, who was the player obstructed. As Emmerich shaped to take it, there was near panic in the English defence. Frantically, Stiles tried to get a wall formed, cursing and dragging his colleagues this way and that. All were shouting, warning: and nobody was properly marking. Emmerich drove the ball, but did not hit it well. It struck Schnellinger on the arm, was glanced down towards the left of Banks's six-yard area, and as Wilson lunged desperately towards it, Weber came round the back of a congestion of six men to strike the ball home. My view at the time, and having studied the video recording, is that Charlton did *not* commit a foul and that Schnellinger's handling was *not* intentional. There was barely time to kick off before Dienst's whistle went for extra time. Boos echoed around the stadium.

Jack Charlton says that when a film of the match was shown to the panel of referees at the next World Cup in Mexico, the majority said that the foul should have been the other way. Schoen reflects that most referees' decisions arouse several opinions: he retained his equanimity whichever way they went. At the moment of the free-kick, Bobby Charlton, totally engrossed in the match, thought there were still about ten minutes to go, and could not believe it when the whistle went almost immediately. It is significant that he thought 'that the system would pull us through', having just subordinated himself to it in one of his most neutral performances ever.

Cohen recounts that Emmerich's free-kick glanced off his knee; while behind him Banks, in those fleeting seconds, could see England's victory disintegrating in a disorganised shambles. 'Well, I had to set a wall up,' he says. 'It was just outside the penalty area. We set it up, Nobby dragging five players in, and there was probably only one of our men on the half-way line. Germany knew it was their last chance of getting back, so they shoved everybody up in the area. Emmerich had a crack, the ball hit the wall and ricocheted out to the left and Schnellinger, pushing forward like everyone else, ran in for the sake of running in, and we thought the ball hit him on the arm. Had it not hit him, it was right out for a throw-in, it wasn't even good for a goal-kick, Emmerich mishit it that badly, Schnellinger's arm took the pace out of it and it just slowly went across as Weber closed in. The ball was on the floor and I thought he might keep it down there until I saw Ray Wilson with his leg stretched out so I dived that little bit higher above Ray's leg in case the ball came off it, but Weber was stretching and he lifted it, and it went over my arm.'

As England turned back up the field to kick off in a mood of disbelief, that Fernandel face of Banks showed little expression. One of the two or three greatest goalkeepers of his time, whose climax was yet to come in Mexico, he was a largish man who tended not to look much like a goalkeeper until the need was upon him. No cat-like nipping about while watching the play upfield, like Bonetti. Banks moved with a slight stoop and a bit of a shuffle, until the moment when he was moving like a trampoline artist to grasp a shot or pluck down a cross from out of the sky. What had just happened was a nightmare, the crowd of players in the six-yard area having made it impossible for him to react in time to Cohen's deflection, Schnellinger's arm or Weber's final lunge. On the bench, Schoen noticed with a certain satisfaction that England's reserves had now been obliged to sit down.

Within seconds the whistle had gone for extra time. Ramsey came out on to the pitch, and Cohen's impression was that he was quite angry, yet through that suppression of emotion he retained his control, and uttered his historic command: 'Look, you've won it once, go out and win it again.' He pointed to the fact that the Germans were feeling the effect of the spongy Wembley turf far more than the English; that, in fatigue, their socks were already rolled down, and that England were morally the stronger. It was a superb, low-key piece of psychology, because not a few of his team were feeling precisely the reverse, aghast at their mistake and believing instinctively that the initiative had now passed to the opposition. Not Ball, however. The red-headed little dynamo was bouncing about, eager to get back into action and take apart the blond German full-back whom he knew to be already near to the point of surrender. 'I just kept saying to myself, "Keep running, keep going, *work*" and when it was all over Alf said to me, "You'll never play better in your life." I was having so much joy out there that day, I knew I could turn the game, that they just couldn't pick me up. I once ran thirty or forty yards in extra time and nearly hit the bar. You don't do that on Wembley's turf. I can remember begging people to give me the ball so that I could run at Schnellinger and put him out of the match. Alf was marvellous, he didn't let us think about any idea of the Germans now being on top, he said we were playing good stuff and that they were not posing a lot of questions, though he was a bit worried about Held making long runs at us on the left.' Schoen was going round his men with the same equanimity as Ramsey. He knew that stability, as much as emotion, would determine the result. 'We felt strong enough to continue playing the same way. We knew it was possible to win. Yet for us to be in extra time, against England at Wembley, was itself a bonus.'

Germany kicked off. Two minutes later, from Ball's corner kick, a shoal of heads went up, the ball dropped free, Bobby Charlton shot from the back of the penalty area and Tilkowski plunged to grasp at the ball by the foot of a post. There could be no arguments about who held the initiative.

Hunt, with his coal-miner's shoulders and long raking stride, was now playing with more assurance than at any time during the first ninety minutes, and he must have seemed awesomely strong to Weber. Breaking on the left, he hit a cross-field shot several yards wide. The clouds had gone, and the late afternoon sun was casting strong shadows on the pitch, dramatising the players' movements. Cohen, pummelling a path down the right, all elbows and knees and kinetic energy, for possibly the only time in the match crossed the ball into no man's land behind the German goal. A minute later England were in front again. Stiles, with fine awareness, lofted a pass down the right beyond Schnellinger for Ball, who turned the ball inside to Hurst. With his back to goal, feinting to go left then swivelling right, Hurst hooked a shot with his right foot, the pivot on his left knee forcing him to lean back and this having the effect of lifting the shot. The ball went like an arrow past Tilkowski, struck the cross-bar, bounced down and up, and was headed behind for a corner by Weber. Had it bounced behind the goal-line? Players of both sides were appealing with gestures, until Dienst was persuaded to go to consult Bakhramov, his Soviet linesman. Though he had been at least ten yards short of the corner flag and therefore had an imperfect view, which may have additionally been obstructed by Ball, Bakhramov, following a brief conversation with Dienst in which the two men could speak no common language, pointed emphatically to the centre spot. A goal. To their lasting credit, the Germans made no more than a token protest.

Beckenbauer, just into the penalty area, had been nearer to the ball than Bakhramov, and with a head-on view. 'It was not a goal,' he says, 'because the ball bounced down and hit the line. That's no goal, you know, the whole ball has to be behind the line. That's the rule. Then the English players jumped about because they thought it's a goal, and we say "No it's not," and then the big discussion comes up and Alan Ball pulls the referee over to the linesman.' The irony is that Ball says he does not think that Bakhramov can have seen it properly. 'I was in a better position than he was and I couldn't really tell myself. It had been a good move leading up to it. Nobby knocked the ball inside the full-back for me and I've got almost to the bye-line and clipped it back, and Hurst has made a near-post run. Because I was worried about being off-side I made to step off the pitch, but as Geoff shot I came back, and as it hit the bar I was right in line with the linesman ten or fifteen yards behind me. As Weber headed over the bar I've turned to the linesman and said "Goal", and there was a lot of schemozzle, and the referee and linesman hardly said a word to each other because they couldn't understand each other, and the linesman just pointed to the centre circle and off he went, but in all honesty, hand on heart, I couldn't say whether it was in or not.'

Bobby Charlton, who has watched re-runs of the film more times than most of us, thinks that it is far from conclusive – 'and probably shows more that it wasn't. My inclination at the time was that it was a goal, because I'd moved forward in case Geoff turned it square to the left, so I was in a reasonable position to see.' His attitude, like Wilson's, was a partial reflection of the action of Hunt. As the ball bounced on or behind the line, Hunt, who lived by taking chances close in, and was at this moment the nearest of all to the ball, had swung around with arms aloft in appeal for a goal. 'Normally in that situation I would have gone in and, looking back, I still don't know why I didn't,' Hunt has said. 'I don't think, in fact, I'd have got the ball. It bounced down and high up to my left and Weber headed it away. I've thought many times since, why did I not go in? The linesman could definitely not have seen. When I looked across moments later, he was still moving back towards the corner flag, he was still so far away and hadn't got his flag up.' Although Hunt's appeal was instinctive and full of professional assurance, it is evident that he was himself far from sure.

Schoen admitted that from the line he could not possibly have an opinion although, like Bobby Charlton, he considered that film suggested it was not a goal and thought that it is possible to detect chalk dust rising as the ball bounces, indicating that the ball hit the line. 'But in that game, the English were better by one goal. It was a great final, and it was a pity that the decisive goal was so controversial. The outstanding thing about that England team was that they had great personalities, a mixture of battlers like Jack Charlton, Stiles and Cohen and the skilful players like Bobby Charlton, Moore and Peters. Alan Ball was not a personality then, but he had great worth for the team in that match. I knew when that third goal was awarded that it would be very difficult to get back into the match. But I was proud of my team – they played very correctly after that goal.'

The stadium was in tumult, the noise deafening as Germany kicked off again. The voguish clapping rhythm of that era, which would continue long into the night on motor-car horns up and down the country, hammered out its jungle beat: *ra-ra*, ra-ra-*ra*, ra-ra-ra-*rah*! A hundred thousand times. If the reverse at the ninetieth minute of the match had been stunning for England, the Germans must now have felt engulfed by the vast wave of opposing emotion. The conventional, restrained English, that strange people across the Channel with their rain-coats and their rain, their bowler hats and their orderly queues of two people at a bus stop, their lack of conversation in public or with people they did not know, were revealing their inner self, that cheerful bawdiness which lay so close beneath the surface; that willing-ness, given the opportunity, to be brash and boastful, which Victorianism had taught them was not the done thing. Out of the shell of moderation, the World Cup hatched an Elizabethan boisterousness of an earlier century: a drinking, uninhibited, almost primitive zest for the moment. Live now, pay later, was the slogan of the time. In the world's most simple and most popular game, the English were winning. And loving it.

Hurst, the young man who had made this all possible, the relative unknown of 24 who had come into the team a few matches before the competition began, who missed the first three matches and was only recalled to replace an injured superstar, felt nothing. The hubbub, he has said, was outside him. 'Inside, there was just a sort of funny, peaceful calm.'

There was no calm for Schnellinger. His head was banging in fatigue as he set off one more time in pursuit of Ball, and the extra-time interval arrived with Emmerich putting a free-kick high over the bar. Wilson had hurried treatment for a blow in the face, suffered two minutes earlier, the whistle went, and there was Ball putting Hunt away on the right. When Hunt was tackled, the player who gathered the loose ball, still a whirlwind of energy after nearly two hours of unrelenting running, was Ball.

Beckenbauer was spent. The same age as Ball, he had run himself into the turf, chasing, shadowing, smothering Charlton. As an England attack rolled towards Tilkowski, Beckenbauer was slowly walking back towards his half of the field. Hunt, as the smallest concession to weariness, rolled his socks down. The enormity of the occasion was injecting strength into Ball's little frame. He rattled through the middle, brought a save out of Tilkowski, took the corner-kick. Germany scrambled the ball away, but it fell to Bobby Charlton at the back of the area, he drove it through a bunch of players, and Tilkowski had to make a late save at the foot of his right-hand post.

With ten minutes remaining one man stood between Germany and defeat: the bustling, quick-footed unpredictable Held, with his blond crew-cut hair. The disintegration of normal tactics suited his style. Now he was surging into the spaces down the left which Emmerich had failed to exploit. Going past Jack Charlton's crabby tackle, he squeezed to the bye-line, hooked the ball waist-high across the goal clear of Banks, but Seeler arrived a fraction too late, and Peters was protecting the far post.

Repeatedly, in the dwindling time available, Held was taking on opponents, running them, feinting: hoping. A cross from the left was headed behind for a corner by Wilson. The rest of Held's team were stooping with fatigue. With one minute to go, Schulz found the strength for a last run on the right, crossed into the goal-mouth, Haller nodded down, and the ball was a shade too far for Seeler to make contact. The ball was heaved back towards the England goal by a German boot; Moore chested it down.

He had been a Herculean figure of the match, and of the whole finals. Youthful and handsome, what he lacked in speed he obscured with his uncanny judgement and anticipation. He moved among opponents like a bank manager among junior clerks, correcting, re-directing and discreetly scolding. He never seemed to be short of time, the hallmark of any great player. Now he gave 1966 the final stamp of his authority. With the stadium full of shrieking whistles demanding 'time', with Dienst looking at his watch but waving play on, Moore took a return pass from Ball . . . back helping in defence! With barely a glance upfield and a shuffle, Moore flighted a pass to the familiar waiting figure of Hurst ten yards into the German half. With false presumption of the end, three spectators were already running on to the pitch as Hurst turned and headed towards goal, the defence falling away from him. His legs were burning, he had little wind left, but he kept going, while Ball, unopposed but unheard on his right, was yelling and yelling, 'Here, square, give it.' Surprised at the absence of challenge, Hurst reached the edge of the penalty area, and with a gesture as much as a shot he thumped the ball at Tilkowski. Possibly because his strength was gone and the shot was half-serious, he struck it perfectly without too much lift or swerve, and it flew into the near top corner of the net. It was the last ball kicked. As the final whistle went, and Hurst swung round to receive the embrace of Peters, Jack Charlton sank to his knees with relief and exhaustion. Whereas Moore hit a glorious last pass, big Jack, that large, angular man who looked capable of carrying a suitcase in each hand and a couple more tucked under either arm, would happily have hoofed the ball instead over the roof to safety: if he could.

'Bobby was unbelievable in that game,' he says. 'He had such control, such presence. In the last minute of the game, balls were bring crossed, and I kept heading. I seemed to head more balls in the last five or ten minutes than in the whole game, as they humped it in. In the last minute, I thought there was going to be a cross to the far post, but it was bent to the near post and Bobby read it, took it on his chest, made for the edge of the box, gave it to Bally, had it back, put his foot on it, had a little look, ran with it a bit, and knocked it over the top to Geoff. And all the time he was doing this, I was screaming, "Kick it over the stern, get rid of it, kick it, kill the bloody thing!" But Bobby played it, and that, as you learn, is the way to play. The more you give the ball away, the more it's going to come back to you. And Bobby didn't give it away, he kept it, and we got the fourth goal, and it was a great moment for me, because it taught me that you have to be able to play from the back.'

As the stadium erupted with a new flood of noise, as the England reserves all leaped to their feet with arms aloft together with Shepherdson and Cocker, a single, expressionless figure still sat on the bench, seemingly impassive in his team's moment of triumph: the ever-enigmatic Ramsey. The story is told, perhaps apocryphally, that he turned to his colleagues and said, 'I do wish you gentlemen would learn to control yourselves.' One can imagine that the smallholder's son from Dagenhem would have greeted the lost explorer of the Nile with the same formality as Stanley's famous 'Dr Livingstone, I presume.' Yet had his team not done what he had said they would? They had fetched him, three and a half years ago, from quiet Ipswich, this taciturn, shy, reserved man, and leading with his chin, as they say, he had promised them victory. There were those who had laughed, and some were still laughing when the tournament began. Now, in the most famous stadium in the game, his name reverberated from the crowd: 'Ram-sey, Ram-sey, Ram-sey . . .'

Armfield was one of those standing just behind Ramsey, the ex-captain who had lost his place and was now cheering with the rest. Only one other man besides Ramsey had a pensive look, yet for a different reason: Greaves. Armfield could recognise Ramsey's mood. 'Alf always lived within himself, he was never the best at showing his feelings. We [the reserves] knew better than the players on the pitch the pressure he was feeling. This was the ultimate, he knew it was that once-in-a-lifetime moment. He was always the one for keeping cool, not counting his chickens.'

'Ee-aye-addio, we won the cup,' the crowd chanted in delirium, again and again and again. Slowly, Ramsey walked forward to shake each of his men by the hand as they moved towards the steps leading up to the Royal Box to collect the trophy. As he reached the top and turned to walk along in front of the VIPs, Moore was worried that his hands were muddy from the wet pitch, and self-consciously wiped them on his shirt and then on the velvet covering of the low wall. 'They were the right colours after all,' the Queen said with a smile, as she handed Moore his medal and the cup.

Hurst followed Moore, smiling broadly, as well he might with those three goals, the first ever hat-trick of a World Cup Final. His name was made for all time. Bobby Charlton looked haggard, lined, and was quietly weeping. Hunt's stoic calm was still with him. Jack Charlton smiled an old player's smile, full of reflection. Ball was laughing a boy's unwitting laugh from ear to ear, Cohen had the old hand's look of accomplishment well earned. Wilson looked pensive, and Peters a little lost. Nobby's toothless grin suggested the cup was all his, while last down the steps and back on to the pitch was the phlegmatic Banks, with that air of the night-watchman. He'd locked the doors.

As the national anthem was struck up, Ramsey dogmatically refused to join his men on their lap of honour. It took my mind back to that spring day in 1963 when I had given him a lift back from Crystal Palace to catch his train home to Ipswich from Liverpool Street station, and he had said, self-effacingly: 'It's not my team, you know, it's England's team.' Right now, England's team was on a spree.

Stiles was doing a sort of African war dance, leaping all over an embarrassed Cohen. 'As we ran round and I looked back and saw Nobby, he looked so funny and I was so emotional, I didn't know whether to laugh or cry,' Jack Charlton says. When Hurst had scored the fourth, Jack had run the length of the pitch to hug him, and just as he got there, Hurst had turned away to put his arm round Peters, and Charlton had sunk to the floor instead. His brother had come up to him and said, 'They can't take that away from us.' It was an emotional moment for the man who had cheated death, though perhaps not as intensely so as two years later when he and his club at last won the European Cup for an even more renowned manager. 'I'd never cried at a match before,' Bobby says, 'but the emotion of the crowd got to me. I suppose you shouldn't cry, really, not over an unimportant thing like a World Cup Final. I was disappointed with my contribution, but staying the whole time with him [Beckenbauer] I guess he felt the same. It was only later I felt disappointed. I'd never stopped running. I thought it might eventually get to the stage where I lost him, but I never shook him off till the last fifteen minutes, when he stayed upfield looking for a goal. He says he's never felt so tired.'

Cohen felt he wanted to walk around on his own, and quietly let the achievement sink in as the crowd continued to throb with glee. He pays tribute to Beckenbauer. 'He did well before the final whistle, trying to get forward, trying to chip the ball up to Seeler, but all the time it was being intercepted and going straight back to his man, Bobby Charlton, who was spraying the ball round everywhere. When it was all over, it was such a relief. It had been such a long season. Fulham had done their usual juggling act to escape relegation, and I'd spent ten days in hospital at the end of the season with an injury. It took time to respond to the size of it all. I really appreciated it. It's the only cup I've ever won.'

Wilson had enjoyed it. After the opening match against Uruguay, it had been more relaxed than he had expected. The two FA Cup finals in which he played, against Sheffield Wednesday and, later, West Bromwich, were far harder, he says, the tournament being strung out from January to May. 'This was all in a fortnight, and because it was so close we stayed in a natural rhythm.'

Back in the dressing-room Ramsey went round, still not showing his emotions, shaking everyone by the hand two or three times again. He clearly felt it very much, 'but he wasn't doing a tango,' as someone put it. Across the corridor, Schoen was congratulating his men on a memorable final in which they had played with spirit and honour. 'I was criticised afterwards for putting Beckenbauer on Charlton, but I would have done it again. They neutralised each other. Beckenbauer didn't yet have so much experience.' Had Schoen left him free to attack, perhaps we should have had ten goals instead of six, the kind of old-time football which from now onwards would become almost extinct. At the Hendon Hall Hotel, extra police had to be called in to keep out the crowd, and, as London went wild with celebrating for the rest of the night, the Government made the insensitive mistake of failing to invite the winning team's wives and girlfriends, whom they had not seen for the past three weeks of intense effort, to the official banquet, which was attended none the less by Pickles's owner. Jack Charlton's wife, Pat, was in hospital expecting a baby, so, after dinner, he went off with a pal from the *Sunday Express*, Jim Mossop, intending to blow two hundred quid. But England was awash with admiration: he didn't have to spend a penny of it as they quietly drank the night away, amid congratulations which would continue for many years.

11

Sundown

THE NEXT DAY, before the squad disbanded to snatch a few days' holiday before the start of the new domestic season, they were invited to lunch at Elstree film studios. Ramsey, in his perverse but endearing manner, told a couple of journalists who asked for his reactions and thoughts for Monday's papers – two of those I may say who had been the most supportive during the months of criticism by the majority – that he was sorry, but he could not give any interviews, because it was his day off! To the troops he was the same as ever. While they were at Elstree he suddenly said, look, he had never talked to them about bonuses, and there was £22,000 to be divided, and how did they want to split it: should it be in proportion to the number of matches they had each played? It was immediately agreed, on Moore's initiative, that as they were a squad, it should be divided straight down the middle, a thousand each. In the hang-over of euphoria, the players hardly paused to consider that for winning the world's most prestigious prize they would be receiving, including match fees, and after the Inland Revenue had dipped its fingers, the modest sum of six or seven hundred pounds. It was only when, later, they learned that the Football Association had paid nearly £240,000 in tax that one or two of them were understandably resentful, with good reason. The losers had been vastly better rewarded, and though finances in English football over the next fifteen years were to become ludicrously out of hand, bringing clubs near to the point of extinction, the FA had not done their players justice.

Yet, almost within hours, worse misjudgements were taking place. At the Royal Garden Hotel on the evening of the victory I had met Bertie Mee, the newly appointed manager of Arsenal and their former physiotherapist, who had been on duty at that boys' coaching course I had attended fifteen years earlier. Five years on, he would guide an Arsenal team using many of the negative trends we had just witnessed in the World Cup to an English Cup and league double. What had he thought of England's victory, I asked? 'Not a bad spectators' game,' he had answered a shade dismissively. It was representative of the new school of thinking we were about to experience.

Almost simultaneously, Len Shipman, the president of the Football League, was saying that the clubs would now have to have the use of their players for summer tours, at the expense of the national team trying to prepare for the European Championship, and for its defence of the world title in Mexico. Over the next two or three years, the impetus of the World Cup would prove to have enormous benefit to League soccer, but the myopia of League officials, together with their blindness to the future dangers of television which they now admitted with ever wider arms, anaesthetised by flattery, was to squander much of the benefit that had been achieved.

There was, widely, the misunderstanding of the manner of England's victory by managers, coaches, theorists and schoolmasters, from the top to the bottom of the game. It was supposed that Ramsey's *system* was wholly responsible, overlooking the quality of the players he had been able to use. In conjunction with the damaging and accelerating growth of the cult of winning, rather than *playing*, coaches who wished to make an impression, managers who wanted to protect their jobs, club directors who lusted for prestige and schoolmasters who corrupted their young pupils into the pursuit of irrelevant junior titles, all conspired to pervert the true course of the game. From now on, a 4-3-3 or 4-4-2 formation was seen to be the Aladdin's lamp to all success.

Even some of the national papers paid empty tribute to England's quality as 'traditional battlers', rather than having the perception to detect that much of the success had hung on the tactical skill and intelligence in the attacking third of the field by Peters, Bobby Charlton, Ball and Hurst. Although it was predictable that headlines in Buenos Aires should refer to 'Lucky Pirates', there were some sceptical voices nearer to home. Karl Rappan, the well known Swiss coach, who had instigated the *libero* system of defence known as the bolt, had written: 'If the match had been played before a crowd of 2,000 for a regional final, some of the players would have been whistled.' Brilliantly though Ramsey's achievement may have been conceived, it had its several and obvious limitations, not least the loss of appeal to the public, on whom the game ultimately depended, with the elimination of wingers, whose role for a century had provided the most conspicuous drama of the game.

Ramsey legitimately defended a triumph which, in a sense, needed no defence. He claimed that the team 'could become one of the greatest of all time', which, but for the aberration in Leon in Mexico in 1970, they might well have gone some of the way to confirming. Following the 1966 defeat of Germany he had said: 'What the foreigners cannot borrow from us is the character of our players and their football intelligence. We haven't the technical level of the Hungarians, though their 1953 team was exceptional. We, and some other teams in the finals, have been called defensive because we have attempted, and succeeded, in stifling opposing individuals. This is what the game is about. It always has been. In 1966, we did it better than anyone else. What's more, using different players at different stages of a match, we attacked more over the whole competition than any other team. We were the fastest and the strongest team, so I don't think we should concentrate on improving these qualities. But I don't think we can match the technique of the Latin Americans or Latin Europeans. We English are built differently.' He added, with that strong streak of patriotism, that he would not now be accepting offers from abroad, of vastly more than his salary of £4,500 a year, because 'I am an Englishman, English football is my life. I can only eat three meals a day and it is what I am doing which counts for me.'

He was caught in the downward spiral of football which 'stifled' the players of opposing teams at the expense of entertainment. These are the totals of goals, and the average per match, of World Cups from the extravagant days of 1954 to 1982:

1954 – 140 (5.38)	*1958* – 117 (3.34)	*1962* – 89 (2.78)
1966 – 89 (2.78)	*1970* – 95 (2.96)	*1974* – 97 (2.55)
1978 – 103 (2.71)	*1982* – 146 (2.80)	

Between 1966 and 1970, whereas Brazil's average per match was 2.5, England's dropped to 1.7. The legacy at the turnstiles was being squandered.

The problem was that Ramsey, along with other prominent professional managers, was tending to lose sight of the point of playing sport, including professional sport. It is, of course, to entertain, to persuade the public to part with money for the privilege of watching. Winning may well be, and very often is, an integral part of that entertainment, but it is by no means all. By handing the game over to the professionals in the Sixties at the upper levels, club and international teams were subjected to the philosophy of the majority of men playing sport for money: play the percentages, reduce the risks, don't take chances. The premise of Mee and his like must ultimately be self-defeating.

Only a few weeks before the FA sacked him in 1974, Ramsey was busy saying, following an exciting friendly against the Scottish League: 'My job is to get results, not to produce entertainment, though of course I would always like to achieve both.' That priority, which almost every professional would uphold, had undermined him and the game, yet the paradox will always exist, as Bobby Moore emphasised when he said: 'Because of success, belief and morale and confidence, all of these grow, and that in itself produces more success.'

Danny Blanchflower knew success, and some failure, as captain of Tottenham and Northern Ireland between 1958 and 1963, yet he has always maintained that football is as much about *glory* as about winning. That of course must be so. There *can* be glorious losers, and it is very often the quality of the loser which helps establish the fame of the winner. As a columnist for the *Sunday Express*, Blanchflower had often been critical of England's performances and of Ramsey's principles during the build-up to 1966, though only with the best intention as one who cared deeply for the game. When he met Ramsey at a Football Writers' Association dinner, Ramsey rounded on him. 'You're a bloody liar. What gives you the right to say what you like?' Ramsey had said, having earlier refused to give Blanchflower an interview. It was an indication of the sensitivity to which Winterbottom has referred.

Ramsey could not accept that the way he chose to play for expediency's sake was not all things to all people. All international team managers are, of course, put under intense and unfair pressure, but that does not excuse all their tactics. Schoen, in his final tournament of 1978, called the World Cup 'a kind of war'; and before the start of the 1966 competition, Ignacio Trelles, the manager of Mexico for his third World Cup, said: 'Alf Ramsey has the worst job of any manager in the Cup. In Mexico in 1970, I don't want anything to do with it.'

Ramsey was both victim and conspirator of the system which now often baffled even the more knowledgeable spectators. 'What happened from 1966 onwards was that full-backs became good on the ball but forgot how to mark, because there were no wingers,' John Connelly says. 'The season after the World Cup, when I was at Blackburn, Keith Newton, our right-back, was always going forward, with no one to mark, and I was expected to be back, kicking off our goal-line. That's what's wrong with the game. It was the same in Rugby League, where I've got relations who were involved with St Helens, and the domination of heavy forwards was killing it, till they introduced the six-tackle law. Now they're busy trying to sell soccer to a public that's disappearing, but who wants to watch goalless draws?'

Professional managers and coaches will always maximise the

advantages available within the existing laws, which is why it was almost criminal that FIFA, the world governing body, persistently resisted any and every attempt to introduce changes to the laws which might have restored some advantage to creative and entertaining players, and reduced negative tactics, until belatedly banning the pass back to the goalkeeper in 1993. It is not sufficient for well-intentioned coaches to say that managers must be positive. With every successive World Cup, the majority of the managers demonstrate that there is little charity towards entertainment; and FIFA that they are exclusively concerned with money.

The first hour of the 1982 World Cup Final was the most disgraceful exhibition of the game by both Italy and West Germany, employing the Ramsey ethic of stifling the opposition to a degree far beyond the laws. Nothing but new legislation could change it. 'In the old days, when I was marking Jimmy Greaves, we'd be on the edge of our penalty box,' Nobby Stiles says, 'but now you're marking a yard inside your own half. The game has no chance.' And as Ian Callaghan observes, 'So many teams copied us after the 1966 that it was a bad thing.'

Fate, however, was particularly cruel on Ramsey in 1970, when Bonetti's errors in Leon threw away a two-goal lead in the semi-final against West Germany. It tends to be forgotten that Beckenbauer's goal, which made it 2-1, was scored before the controversial substitution of Bell for Bobby Charlton. Had England reached the final against Brazil, which in all probability they would have otherwise done, Ramsey would have laid to rest the accusation of 1966 that his team was capable only of playing at Wembley, when he had in fact produced the first team, and to an extent the last, which performed equally efficiently on foreign soil. His own obstinacy, tending to prefer destructive players such as Storey rather than exciting crowd pleasers such as Channon – who is still England's tenth most prolific scorer of all time – and his unfailingly dismal public relations, thereafter saw his star decline.

He clumsily turned the media against him when, returning from Mexico, he made his now celebrated comment that 'we have nothing to learn from Brazil'; when, as we know, what he meant was that England could not usefully try to copy the characteristics of the Brazilian game. He said he was unaware of being rude to people, yet his maladroit utterances were well known: such as the time when, watching a boys' match at Portman Road, he was invited down to the boardroom by John Cobbold to join the directors, who were still celebrating the winning of the championship. 'No, thank you,' said Ramsey, 'I'm working.'

Ray Wilson, who was always one of the most reticent of players off the pitch, recognised Ramsey's limited tact, however much he admired him as a manager. 'I could understand the criticism of our play in the World Cup, because we didn't make the ball talk, like Portugal or Brazil, and I could see why people felt that Alf was very stand-offish and a bit abrupt, curt. I think that was generally with press people, and I don't say he was right on that count. I think he was a little bit too stand-offish. He was totally protective of his players, and it was really about keeping the press away from the lads. When you think that during the World Cup we were together something like six or seven weeks and he only allowed the press near us a couple of times, I'm sure that wouldn't help him very much with the press.'

It was much different from the open house which was given by the Dutch in 1974, by Argentina in 1978 and regularly by the Brazilians. So when results started to go against Ramsey in 1973 – he won only two of his last eight matches – he had no access to a press platform which might have helped him stall a growing dissatisfaction within the FA. Sadly, that disenchantment had more to do with worry at the loss of finances from failing to qualify for the World Cup in 1974, than with the image of the game. Had Ramsey possessed the outward amiability of Schoen, he might well have remained manager for longer, but he always found it difficult to establish a working relationship with the amateurs of Lancaster Gate. In 113 international matches he suffered only 17 defeats. Cohen, as loyal as the rest of the squad, calls Ramsey's sacking 'administrative vandalism'. What must be said in his defence is that, like Revie, Greenwood and Robson who were to follow him, he suffered from the continual obstruction of the League and their clubs, who make it doubly hard for an England manager to make adequate preparation of the team which carries the national flag.

Whatever the aftermath of 1966, what will never be forgotten is that Ramsey welded, by a combination of his and their personalities and application, a marvellously synchronised unit, who loved him then and still do. If he was a stern task-master, that was part of his strength, allied to his fairness: everyone appreciates discipline, and that factor is too often absent in most walks of life today. Nobody, under Alf, ever took his place for granted. 'It was one thing Alf made sure you didn't do,' Banks says. 'It was one of his strong points, really, because you were always fighting for your place. I recall a time we'd played at Wembley, and were returning home on Thursday. Alf had this point that he would always thank people whether they had played in the match or not, thank them for coming and being part of it. I think there were about four or five of us catching a train north, and he'd laid on a bus to take us to the station, and we were checking out of the hotel, he turned to me and put his hand out, and I sort of said, "Thanks very much, Alf, I'll see you," and with a dead straight face he said, "Will you?" But if I hadn't had the accident [a car crash in 1972, in which he lost an eye] I'm certain I could have played for quite a while longer.' If it was arguable in 1966 whether Banks was superior to Yashin, the veteran Russian, Mazurkieviez of Uruguay or Albertosi of Italy, there was no doubt that by 1970 he was the undisputed best in the world: unflappable, undemonstrative, and with an astonishing positional sense; and Ramsey's first choice for nine years until he lost his eye.

Cohen played seven more internationals after the World Cup, and then ruined his knee, stretching to reach a ball before Peter Thompson when playing for Fulham against Liverpool, and after a prolonged and unavailing attempt to regain fitness was finished at the age of 29: a one-club man. A much worse crisis was to overtake him when he discovered in the early Seventies that he had stomach cancer, to which he reacted with the same clear-headed fortitude that had distinguished his playing career. Harrowing chemotherapy and a colostomy by-pass operation were endured, and with the devotion of his wife and the diligence of surgeons he recovered, to continue to lead an active life as a property developer in Kent.

A convivial and uncomplicated man, he enjoyed his time. 'If anyone remembers me now,' he says with a smile, 'it's because I attacked down the wing such a lot. I'd prefer to be remembered as a full-back whom wingers found hard to beat!'

Jack Charlton continued, as player and then manager, to be noted as one who always spoke his mind. At a pre-World Cup training session at Highbury he once told Ramsey he was 'talking a load of crap', to which an unperturbed Ramsey politely replied that, whatever Charlton might think, that was the way it was going to be. Dropped, in favour of Labone – of which he also disapproved – Charlton made 629 league appearances for Leeds over 22 seasons, before retiring with a testimonial attended by a crowd of 34,000. In a total of 770 appearances for the first team he scored, for a centre-half, an exceptional 96 goals, having become at the same time an outstanding qualified coach. He revived Middlesbrough, with some controversially defensive play, and then Sheffield Wednesday, before joining Newcastle in 1984 and abruptly walking out a year later when the crowd showed their displeasure before the season had even begun. He thinks his outspoken views probably robbed him of any chance of being considered for the English post when Revie shamefully quit for a bag of Arab swag in 1977. 'I was annoyed I was not even interviewed,' he says, 'and didn't even get a reply to the application I made. I've got too many strong views, and I tend to challenge accepted opinions.' His subsequent management of the Republic of Ireland team at two World Cup Finals was both a story of romance and a reflection of many of the pragmatic attitudes of Ramsey.

Football, he says, is a matter of memories, as much about the good matches you lose as the ones you win. 'It's like the fish you lose, not the ones you land! The ones that get away are the memory.' He reflects that playing for England, because the team was so good, he spent much of the time watching the match. 'In league football, people come at you fast all the time, you're constantly competing for space. With England, you're always waiting, checking in and checking out, it's slower, there's more thinking, you have to make sure people never get behind you. My responsibility was to go for everything in the air, me on the far post, Bobby Moore on the near post, just a nod between us that worked very well. Bob not only read the game, he read *me* too. All I had to do was make sure the opposition didn't get the ball, never mind whether I did.'

Bobby Moore's career ended with his one thousandth senior match, playing for Fulham against Blackburn in 1977, having played a record 108 times for England. For some years he faded into the half-light of the game, playing in America and Hong Kong, briefly managing Oxford City in the Isthmian League, eventually being invited to pick up the reins at modest and troubled Southend United in 1984. It was strange, some considered, that the FA never took the chance to use his enormous respect internationally to help promote the game, but Moore himself held no grudge at the absence of offers when he was first available. He was a classic example of the creative defender who had utilised all his strengths to overcome his deficiencies in speed. Like Denis Law and so many of the older generation, he had studiously worked at his skills and every aspect of the game as an apprentice. 'Bobby was marvellous on the ground and a greater reader of the ball,' Cohen says. 'He would have you on a piece of string, he would send you out, hold you back, give you advice, clean up behind you, with wonderful distribution of the game.'

Moore enjoyed learning the ropes at Southend. 'Everyone seemed more surprised than I was that I didn't immediately get offered a job. Because you succeed as a player there's no guarantee you'll do it as a manager. Whoever you are, you start from square one. It's easy to have an opinion about a decision, when your opinions don't count. Of course I lost some time for developing as a manager because I carried on playing for so long, whereas John Lyall, say, had to pack up because of an injury at 23, and was straight into learning the business from the bottom, under Ron at West Ham. I have no regrets, though I had my full badge from the FA for coaching by the time I was 21.'

He considered the level of national ability was down; that the desire and commitment were the same, but not the depth of boys who were interested. 'There are so many alternatives today. I'd not been in a squash or golf club till I turned pro! We never had the same opportunities they have today. You probably didn't have a car. If you wanted to play golf, it was probably two buses, a train and a bloody long walk. If you went out, it was once a week if you were lucky, to the pictures or snooker. Mostly, you were filling in time, sitting around tables having cups of tea, an hour's talk, *absorbing*. The chance is still there today, if you want to *make* it there. In the depths of winter, I used to spend the time lobbing a tennis ball up the stairs and controlling it as it bounced down. All learning comes from repetitive work. Practice doesn't necessarily make perfect. It just makes permanent, so the work has to be correct. It's no different from tennis or golf, where the pros spend *hours* practising.'

Ray Wilson was another definitive hard-working professional, thirty of whose 63 caps were gained while he was in the Second Division with Huddersfield. When he retired at 34 with Everton, he had never had his name taken in a league match – a remarkable tribute to someone who was a tenacious tackler. His last international was the third place match against Russia in the 1968 European Championship in Rome. He briefly tried management with Bradford, who vainly offered him five times as much money to stay on as he would get from taking over from his father-in-law in a small undertakers' business near Halifax. He goes lake walking for pleasure nowadays, and is glad he's detached from the game. 'Football on television doesn't keep me in these days, though I didn't watch that many games when I was playing. I had twenty years doing something marvellous, instead of being down a pit. I'd started as a waggon repairer at Shirebrook, near Mansfield. I don't envy them their money today. What about the likes of great players like Carter and Doherty, who played for peanuts? It's now that I realise how good the 1966 squad was, how comfortable we were. When we had the Bradford charity match for the fire, it was just as if I was going down to Wembley again. There was a feeling in those days that you had a gift, and you didn't abuse it. There were no handshakes or testimonials when I retired. I wasn't a public player, but what I had from my career was superb. Winning the World Cup would have been better for my career had I been younger, like Ball or Peters. It had to make you a *better* player, so long as you kept your living right. It means more to me now than it did at the time.'

Nobby Stiles admits that he enjoyed it so much, he was obliged to tell white lies to his wife to disguise it. 'You know, I'd make out I didn't want to, but "I've got to go to Hendon for another three days." It was fantastic to be a part of it, all those characters. We had four world class players, Banks, Wilson, and the two Bobbys, but there was no big-headedness. The terrific thing was we just knew we weren't going to get beaten.' From Manchester United, Stiles went to join Jack Charlton, at Middlesbrough, was then with Bobby Charlton at Preston, subsequently became manager, and in 1958 succeeded Johnny Giles, his brother-in-law, as manager of a struggling West Bromwich Albion; replaced, only months later, by Ron Saunders.

Alan Ball, thrown out as a boy by Bolton for being too small, buzzed around the clubs like he buzzed around the field: from Blackpool to Everton, on to Arsenal, Southampton, to America; to Blackpool, as manager, where he was soon sacked, back to Southampton, as player with Lawrie McMenemy; then, 'to learn the trade', as youth team coach at Portsmouth. In 1995 he was given the responsibility of trying to rescue Manchester City. He won 72 caps, and thinks, inimitably, 'it should have been a hundred', if Revie had not dropped him after recalling him as captain in 1974-75. 'I'd been a runner before the World Cup in 1966, but from then on, my new reputation made me a marked man when I moved to Everton. I had to become a one-touch player. The next season, I always had someone on me: Bremner, Yorath, Storey, Stiles. The World Cup made me a better player, I had to learn again, which is why I played till I was 38. I wouldn't have done otherwise. If the World Cup had happened to me later, I'd have been a millionaire! I'd have liked it to happen later, not for the money. I couldn't *measure* it at the time. It was special, yet it meant nothing. I got in the car and went home. I would have loved it to have happened at 30. There was talk of Juventus wanting me. The world was at my feet. What I gained was what I learned from Bobby Moore. He had so much brain, compensating for his lack of pace. He could sense danger way in advance. He was uncanny. So I tried to reverse that, to see *creativity* early.'

Bobby Charlton was a nonpareil. You could walk up a hill in Albania and find boys kicking a ball around, as I once did, and they had heard of Bobbee Charlton. If Peters was ahead of his time, Bobby was out of any time: a genius, and always a joy to behold. If George Best was the most technically complete British player I ever saw, Bobby gave me the most pleasure. How many know him today? He tells the tale of the small boy at one of his coaching classes, who came up to him and said, 'My grandad used to watch you play when he was little.' Abroad, he is to British sport what Churchill was to politics. 'He was,' says Armfield, 'our trump.' Charlton says that though the World Cup was not the end of his career, after that there was nothing to aim at. 'I'd like to have won away from home in Mexico, but having said that, everything was an anti-climax after 1966. It was the end of any ambition you ever had. From the time you first realise you have ability, you're looking to get picked for the school team, the local team, the area, the county, the English schools team, then will you make it as a pro, will you get selected for England? The World Cup is the end of the line.' His brother puts his finger on the balance of 1966. 'Bobby was the difference between our being average and being good,' Jack says.

Martin Peters, like Ball, was too young to appreciate the full impact of the victory. Had his goal, which made it 2-1, been the winner, his reputation would have added status, yet he does not feel cheated of the honour which passed instead to Hurst. 'I was only concerned with winning the game. I was very naive, I just wanted to play well. It was great to be there, three months previously I'd been relatively unknown. For me, the Brazil match in 1970 was the best. They had a bad defence, yet the way they played you could never get at it! I didn't leave West Ham for Tottenham because I felt in the shadow of Bobby and Geoff, as some people thought, but because I'd been there eleven years, and at 26 I wanted to be part of a side which was going to win things. I'd become disillusioned with their football.'

From Spurs, Peters went to Norwich, later became manager of Sheffield United, and subsequently worked, together with Hurst, for a Dagenham firm of motor insurers, happily establishing a new career.

When Bill Shankly dropped Hunt, he decided reluctantly to move to Bolton. It was a sad time and did not last long. 'I'd hoped I would be able to finish my career with Liverpool, and when I got left out I was still the leading scorer, so it hurt a bit.' But he was fortunate to have in the background a transport business, which his father and uncle had begun, and when he went out of the game he had a ready-made occupation into which to sink his energies. He and his brother bought out his uncle, and now, though by no means wealthy, he has a thriving company. He stayed in touch for a while through his involvement in the pools panel, travelling to London every Friday evening, from November to March, to be on stand-by in case the weather should disrupt the coupon, and he and his colleagues, including former referee Arthur Ellis, had to decide if Exeter would have won away to Hartlepool.

Geoff Hurst has tried to live his life not by being remembered for his hat-trick. He became a centre-forward of exceptional positional sense and developed a fine understanding in 1970 with Francis Lee: feared, indeed, by Brazil. Matt Busby once offended Greenwood by publicly 'tapping' Hurst with a £200,000 offer, at the time a record, to which Greenwood had replied cryptically, by telegram: 'No. Greenwood.' Eventually, Hurst moved to Stoke, then as player-manager to Telford, and thence as manager to

Chelsea. The touch did not last. History will rank him, under far more physical pressure, as good in the air as Lawton, little short of Lofthouse and Milburn in tenacity, and tactically more astute than all three.

The last word I would like to leave with John Connelly, from the breed of forgotten wingers, the men who suddenly ceased to matter after 1966. 'The World Cup squad was great, no backbiting, *everyone* was behind the success. If you have a good dressing-room, you'll have a good team. All I miss now is the dressing-room.'

There lay the real story of the boys of '66. The irony of England's last glory is that it heralded an era of unprecedented international club success which in turn generated a mindless minority of deranged spectators who could not bear to lose. The hooligan mob, a minority numbering only hundreds but nonetheless potentially lethal, for twenty years were to deface cities at home and abroad, culminating with the Heysel disaster in Brussels in 1985, with thirty-nine deaths immediately prior to kick-off in the European Cup Final between Liverpool and Juventus of Turin. With the even worse tragedy at Hillsborough, Sheffield in 1988, at the FA Cup semi-final between Liverpool and Nottingham Forest, with ninety-eight crushed to death – caused not by crowd violence but errant policing of a huge crowd impatient to gain access into an outdated stadium with the game already having begun – sanity thereafter belatedly returned to football terraces, aided by the Inquiry and preventive regulations demanded by Lord Justice Taylor.

Up to now, however, England's former world mastery on the field has continued to remain elusive. Whether Sven Goran Eriksson can harness, in the summer of 2006, some genuine but too often wayward talents, among which the tempestuous Wayne Rooney is an undoubted potential match winner, remains to be seen. The founding nation of the game eagerly awaits the outcome.

Whatever England were to achieve in Germany in the summer of 2006, it was essential that they should conduct themselves with good grace, on and off the field, thereby repairing some of the loss of face suffered from the inept and improper bidding campaign to host those championships – for which there had been a known gentleman's agreement that the World Cup of 2006 would be staged by Germany – and the poor sportsmanship of complaints about a disallowed goal in the semi-final of Euro '04 against Portugal, which encouraged mindless supporters to mount a hate campaign against the unfortunate referee. The Football Association, founding fathers of the game's organisation, once stood above such behaviour, and it is imperative that they should now be seen to return to former standards of ethics.

APPENDIX

World Cup Final Competition 1966

Full Results and Teams

First Round

Group I

ENGLAND 0, URUGUAY 0 (0-0)   *Wembley, 11 July*

ENGLAND
Banks, Cohen, Wilson, Stiles, J. Charlton, Moore, Ball, Greaves, R. Charlton, Hunt, Connelly

URUGUAY
Mazurkieviez, Troche, Manicera, Goncalvez, Caetano, Cortes, Rocha, Perez, Ubinas, Viera, Silva

Referee: I. Zsolt (Hungary)
Attendance 75,000

FRANCE 1, MEXICO 1 (0-0)   *Wembley, 13 July*

FRANCE
Aubour, Djorkaeff, de Michele, Artelesa, Budzinski, Bosquier, Combin, Bonnel, Gondet, Herbin, Hausser

MEXICO
Calderon, Chaires, Pena, Nunez, Hernandez, Diaz, Mercado, Reyes, Borja, Fragoso, Padilla

Referee: M. Ashkenasi (Israel). *Scorers:* Hausser (France)
                                      Borja (Mexico)
Attendance 55,000

URUGUAY 2, FRANCE 1 (2-1)   *White City, 15 July*

URUGUAY
Mazurkieviez, Troche, Manicera, Goncalvez, Caetano, Cortes, Rocha, Perez, Ubinas, Viera, Sacia

FRANCE
Aubour, Djorkaeff, Artelesa, Budzinski, Bosquier, Bonnel, Simon, Herbet, de Bourgoing, Gondet, Hausser

Referee: K. Galba (Czech). *Scorers:* Rocha, Cortes (Uruguay)
                                      de Bourgoing (France)
Attendance 40,000

ENGLAND 2, MEXICO 0 (1-0)   *Wembley, 16 July*

ENGLAND
Banks, Cohen, Wilson, Stiles, J. Charlton, Moore, Paine, Greaves, R. Charlton, Hunt, Peters

MEXICO
Calderon, Chaires, Pena, Del Muro, Jauregui, Diaz, Padilla, Nunez, Borja, Reyes, Hernandez

Referee: C.Lo Bello (Italy). *Scorers:* R. Charlton, Hunt
Attendance 85,000

URUGUAY 0, MEXICO 0 (0-0)   *Wembley, 19 July*
URUGUAY
Mazurkieviez, Troche, Manicera, Ubinas, Goncalvez, Caetano, Cortes, Viera, Sacia, Rocha, Perez

MEXICO
Carbajal, Chaires, Pena, Nunez, Hernandez, Diaz, Mercado, Reyes, Cisneros, Borja, Padilla

Referee: B. Loow (Sweden)
Attendance 35,000

ENGLAND 2, FRANCE 0 (1-0)   *Wembley, 20 July*
ENGLAND
Banks, Cohen, Wilson, Stiles, J. Charlton, Moore, Callaghan, Greaves, R. Charlton, Hunt, Peters

FRANCE
Aubour, Djorkaeff, Artelesa, Budzinski, Bosquier, Bonnel, Herbin, Simon, Herbet, Gondet, Hausser

Referee: A. Yamasaki (Peru). *Scorer:* Hunt (2)
Attendance 92,500

	P	W	D	L	F	A	Pts
England	3	2	1	0	4	0	5
Uruguay	3	1	2	0	2	1	4
Mexico	3	0	2	1	1	3	2
France	3	0	1	2	2	5	1

Group II

WEST GERMANY 5, SWITZERLAND 0 (3-0)   *Hillsborough, 12 July*
WEST GERMANY
Tilkowski, Höttges, Schnellinger, Beckenbauer, Weber, Brülls, Schulz, Haller, Seeler, Overath, Held

SWITZERLAND
Elsener, Grobety, Schneiter, Tacchella, Fuhrer, Bani, Durr, Odermatt, Kunzli, Hosp, Schindelholz

Referee: H. Phillips (Scotland). *Scorers:* Held, Haller (2), Beckenbauer (2)
Attendance 36,000

ARGENTINA 2, SPAIN 1 (0-0)   *Villa Park, 13 July*
ARGENTINA
Roma, Perfumo, Marzolini, Ferriero, Rattin, Albrecht, Solari, Gonzalez, Artimé, Onega, Mas

SPAIN
Iribar, Sanchis, Silvestre, Martinez, Fernandez, Zoco, Ufarte, Del Sol, Peiro, Suarez, Gento

Referee: D. Roumentchev (Bulgaria). *Scorers:* Artimé (2) (Argentina)
                                        Martinez (Spain)
Attendance 42,738

SPAIN 2, SWITZERLAND 1 (1-0)   *Hillsborough, 15 July*
SPAIN
Iribar, Sanchis, Reija, Martinez, Fernandez, Zoco, Amaro, Del Sol, Peiro, Suarez, Gento

SWITZERLAND
Elsener, Fuhrer, Brodmann, Leimgruber, Stierli, Bani, Kuhn, Gottardi, Armbruster, Hosp, Quentin

Referee: T. Bakhramov (Russia). *Scorers:* Sanchis, Amaro (Spain)
Quentin (Switzerland)
Attendance 32,000

ARGENTINA 0, WEST GERMANY 0 (0-0)   *Villa Park, 16 July*
ARGENTINA
Roma, Perfumo, Marzolini, Ferreiro, Rattin, Albrecht, Solari, Gonzalez, Artimé, Onega, Mas

WEST GERMANY
Tilkowski, Höttges, Schnellinger, Beckenbauer, Schulz, Weber, Brülls, Haller, Seeler, Overath, Held

Referee: K. Zecevic (Yugoslavia)
Attendance 46,587

ARGENTINA 2, SWITZERLAND 0 (0-0)   *Hillsborough, 19 July*
ARGENTINA
Roma, Perfumo, Marzolini, Ferreiro, Calics, Rattin, Solari, Gonzalez, Artimé, Onega, Mas

SWITZERLAND
Eichmann, Fuhrer, Brodmann, Stierli, Armbruster, Bani, Kuhn, Gottardi, Hosp, Kunzil, Quentin

Referee: J. F. Campos (Portugal). *Scorers:* Artimé, Onega
Attendance 32,127

WEST GERMANY 2, SPAIN 1 (1-1)   *Villa Park, 20 July*
WEST GERMANY
Tilkowski, Höttges, Schnellinger, Beckenbauer, Schulz, Weber, Kraemer, Seeler, Held, Overath, Emmerich

SPAIN
Iribar, Sanchis, Reija, Glaria, Fernandez, Zoco, Amaro, Rodriguez, Martinez, Fuste, Lapetra

Referee: A. Marques (Brazil). *Scorers:* Emmerich, Seeler (West Germany)
Fuste (Spain)
Attendance 45,187

	P	W	D	L	F	A	Pts
West Germany	3	2	1	0	7	1	5
Argentina	3	2	1	0	4	1	5
Spain	3	1	0	2	4	5	2
Switzerland	3	0	0	3	1	9	0

Group III

BRAZIL 2, BULGARIA 0 (1-0)   *Goodison Park, 12 July*
BRAZIL
Gylmar, D. Santos, Bellini, Altair, P. Henrique, Denilson, Lima, Garrincha, Alcindo, Pelé, Jairzinho

BULGARIA
Naidenov, Shalamanov, Penev, Vutzov, Gaganelov, Kitov, Zhechev, Dermendijev, Asparoukhov, Yakimov, Kolev

Referee: K. Tschenscher (W Germany). *Scorers:* Pelé, Garrincha
Attendance 47,308

PORTUGAL 3, HUNGARY 1 (1-0)   *Old Trafford, 13 July*
PORTUGAL
Carvalho, Morais, Baptista, Lucas, Hilario, Graca, Coluna, Augusto, Eusebio, Torres, Simoes

HUNGARY
Szentmihalyi, Matrai, Kaposzta, Sovari, Meszoly, Sipos, Bené, Nagy, Albert, Farkas, Rakosi

Referee: L. Callaghan (Wales). *Scorers:* Augusto (2), Torres (Portugal)
Bené (Hungary)
Attendance 29,866

HUNGARY 3, BRAZIL 1 (1-1) *Goodison Park, 15 July*
HUNGARY
Gelet, Matrai, Kaposzta, Meszoly, Sipos, Szepesi, Mathesz, Rakosi, Bené, Albert, Farkas

BRAZIL
Gylmar, D. Santos, Bellini, Altair, P. Henrique, Gerson, Tostao, Lima, Garrincha, Alcindo, Jairinho

Referee: K. Dagnall (England). *Scorers:* Bené, Farkas, Meszoly (Hungary)
Tostao (Brazil)
Attendance 51,387

PORTUGAL 3, BULGARIA 0 (2-0) *Old Trafford, 16 July*
PORTUGAL
Pereira, Festa, Figueiredo, Lucas, Hilario, Graca, Coluna, Augusto, Eusebio, Torres, Simoes

BULGARIA
Naidenov, Shalamanov, Penev, Vutzov, Gaganelov, Zhechev, Yakimov, Dermendjiev, Zhekov, Asparoukhov, Rostov

Referee: J. M. Codesal (Uruguay). *Scorers:* Vutzov (own goal), Eusebio, Torres
Attendance 25,438

PORTUGAL 3, BRAZIL 1 (2-0) *Goodison Park, 19 July*
PORTUGAL
Pereira, Morais, Baptista, Lucas, Hilario, Graca, Coluna, Augusto, Eusebio, Torres, Simoes

BRAZIL
Manga, Fidelis, Brito, Orlando, Rildo, Denilson, Lima, Jairzinho, Silva, Pelé, Parana

Referee: G. McCabe (England). *Scorers:* Simoes, Eusebio (2) (Portugal)
Rildo (Brazil)
Attendance 58,479

HUNGARY 3, BULGARIA 1 (2-1) *Old Trafford, 20 July*
HUNGARY
Gelei, Kaposzta, Matrai, Szepesi, Meszoly, Sipos, Mathesz, Bené, Albert, Farkas, Rakosi

BULGARIA
Simeonov, Largov, Penev, Vutzov, Gaganelov, Zhechev, Davidov, Asparoukhov, Kolev, Yakimov, Kotkov

Referee: R. Giocoechea (Argentina). *Scorers:* Davidov (own goal), Meszoly,
Bené (Hungary)
Asparoukhov (Bulgaria)
Attendance 24,129

	P	W	D	L	F	A	Pts
Portugal	3	3	0	0	9	2	6
Hungary	3	2	0	1	7	5	4
Brazil	3	1	0	2	4	6	2
Bulgaria	3	0	0	3	1	8	0

Group IV

U.S.S.R. 3, NORTH KOREA 0 (2-0)   *Ayresome Park, 12 July*
U.S.S.R.
Kavazashvili, Ponomarev, Shesternev, Khurtsilava, Ostrovskiy, Sabo, Sichinava, Chislenko, Banishevskiy, Malofeev, Khusainov

NORTH KOREA
Li Chan Myung, Pak Li Sup, Shin Yung Kyoo, Lim, Zoong Sun, Kang Bong Chil, Pak Seung Zin, Im Seung Hwi, Han Bong Zim, Pak Doo Ik, Kang Ryong Woon, Kim Seung II

Referee: J. Gardeazabal (Spain). *Scorers:* Malofeev (2), Banishevskiy
Attendance 23,006

ITALY 2, CHILE 0 (1-0)   *Roker Park, 13 July*
ITALY
Albertosi, Burgnich, Rosato, Salvadore, Facchetti, Bulgarelli, Lodetti, Perani, Mazzola, Rivera, Barison

CHILE
Olivares, Eyzaguirre, Cruz, Figueroa, Villanueva, Prieto, Marcos, Araya, Tobar, Fouilloux, Sanchez

Referee: G. Dienst (Switzerland). *Scorers:* Mazzola, Barison
Attendance 27,199

NORTH KOREA 1, CHILE 1 (0-1)   *Ayresome Park, 15 July*
NORTH KOREA
Li Chan Myung, Pak Li Sup, Shin Yung Kyoo, Lim Zoong Sun, Oh Yoon Kyung, Pak Seung Zin, Im Seung Hwi, Han Bong Zin, Pak Doo Ik, Li Dong Woon, Kim Seung II

CHILE
Olivares, Valentini, Cruz, Figueroa, Villanueva, Prieto, Marcos, Fouilloux, Landa, Araya, Sanchez

Referee: A. Kandil (U.A.R.). *Scorers:* Pak Seung Zin (N. Korea)
                                    Marcos (Chile)
Attendance 13,792

U.S.S.R. 1, ITALY 0 (1-0)   *Roker Park, 16 July*
U.S.S.R.
Yashin, Ponomarev, Shesternev, Khurtsilava, Danilov, Sabo, Voronin, Chislenko, Malofeev, Banishevskiy, Khusainov

ITALY
Albertosi, Bulgarelli, Burgnich, Facchetti, Leoncini, Lodetti, Mazzola, Meroni, Pascutti, Rosato, Salvadore

Referee: R. Kreitlein (West Germany). *Scorer:* Chislenko
Attendance 27,793

NORTH KOREA 1, ITALY 0 (1-0)   *Ayresome Park, 19 July*
NORTH KOREA
Li Chan Myung, Lim Zoong Sun, Shin Yung Kyoo, Ha lung Won, Oh Yoon Kyung, Im Seung Hwi, Pak Seung Zin, Han Bong Zin, Pak Doo Ik, Kim Bong Hwan, Yang Sung Kook

ITALY
Albertosi, Landini, Janich, Guarneri, Facchetti, Bulgarelli, Fogli, Perani, Mazzola, Rivera, Barison

Referee: P. Schwinte (France). *Scorer:* Pak Doo Ik
Attendance 17,829

U.S.S.R. 2, CHILE 1 (1-1) *Roker Park, 20 July*
U.S.S.R.
Kavazashvili, Getmanov, Shesternev, Korneev, Ostrovskiy, Voronin, Afonin, Metreveli, Serebrjannikov, Markarov, Porkujan

CHILE
Olivares, Valentini, Cruz, Figueroa, Villanueva, Marcos, Prieto, Araya, Landa, Yavar, Sanchez

Referee: J.D. Adair (Northern Ireland). *Scorers:* Porkujan (2) (U.S.S.R.)
Marcos (Chile)
Attendance 16,027

	P	W	D	L	F	A	Pts
U.S.S.R.	3	3	0	0	6	1	6
North Korea	3	1	1	1	2	4	3
Italy	3	1	0	2	2	2	2
Chile	3	0	1	2	2	5	1

Quarter-Finals
23 July

ENGLAND 1, ARGENTINA 0 (0-0) *Wembley*
ENGLAND
Banks, Cohen, Wilson, Stiles, J. Charlton, Moore, Ball, Hurst, R. Charlton, Hunt, Peters

ARGENTINA
Roma, Ferreiro, Perfumo, Albrecht, Marzolini, Rattin, Solari, Gonzalez, Artimé, Onega, Mas

Referee: R. Kreitlein (W. Germany). *Scorer:* Hurst
Attendance 88,000

WEST GERMANY 4, URUGUAY 0 (1-0) *Hillsborough*
WEST GERMANY
Tilkowski, Höttges, Schnellinger, Weber, Schulz, Haller, Beckenbauer, Overath, Seeler, Held, Emmerich

URUGUAY
Mazurkieviez, Troche, Manicera, Ubinas, Goncalvez, Caetano, Salva, Rocha, Silva, Cortes, Perez

Referee: J. Finney (England). *Scorers:* Held, Beckenbauer, Seeler, Haller
Attendance 40,000

PORTUGAL 5, NORTH KOREA 3 (2-3) *Goodison Park*
PORTUGAL
Pereira, Morais, Baptista, Lucas, Hilario, Graca, Coluna, Augusto, Eusebio, Torres, Simoes

NORTH KOREA
Li Chan Myung, Lim Zoong Sun, Shin Yung Kyoo, Ha Jung Won, Oh Yoon Kyung, Pak Seung Zin, Im Seung Hwi, Han Bong Zin, Pak Doo Ik, Li Dong Woon, Yang Sung Kook

Referee: M. Ashkenasi (Israel). *Scorers:* Eusebio (4) (2 pen.), Augusto
(Portugal)
Pak Seung Zin, Li Dong Woon,
Yang Sung Kook (N. Korea)

Attendance 40,248

U.S.S.R. 2, HUNGARY 1 (1-0) *Roker Park*
U.S.S.R.
Yashin, Ponomarev, Shesternev, Voronin, Danilov, Sabo, Khusainov, Chislenko, Banishevskiy, Malofeev, Porkujan

HUNGARY
Gelei, Kaposzta, Szepesi, Meszoly, Matrai, Sipos, Nagy, Bené, Albert, Farkas, Rakosi

Referee: J. Gardeazabal (Spain). *Scorers:* Chislenko, Porkujan (U.S.S.R.)
Bené (Hungary)
Attendance 22,103

Semi-Finals

WEST GERMANY 2, U.S.S.R. 1 (1-0)　　　　　　*Goodison Park, 25 July*
WEST GERMANY
Tilkowski, Lutz, Schnellinger, Weber, Schulz, Haller, Beckenbauer, Overath, Seeler, Held, Emmerich

U.S.S.R.
Yashin, Ponomarev, Shesternev, Voronin, Danilov, Sabo, Khusainov, Chislenko, Banishevskiy, Malofeev, Porkujan

Referee: C. Lo Bello (Italy). *Scorers:* Haller, Beckenbauer (W. Germany)
Porkujan (U.S.S.R.)
Attendance 38,273

ENGLAND 2, PORTUGAL 1 (1-0)　　　　　　*Wembley, 26 July*
ENGLAND
Banks, Cohen, Wilson, J. Charlton, Moore, Stiles, R. Charlton, Peters, Ball, Hurst, Hunt

PORTUGAL
Pereira, Festa, Baptista, Carlos, Hilario, Graca, Coluna, Augusto, Eusebio, Torres, Simoes

Referee: P. Schwinte (France). *Scorers:* R. Charlton (2) (England)
Eusebio (pen.) (Portugal)
Attendance 90,000

3rd Place Match

PORTUGAL 2, U.S.S.R. 1 (1-1)　　　　　　*White City, 29 July*
PORTUGAL
Pereira, Festa, Baptista, Carlos, Hilario, Graca, Coluna, Augusto, Eusebio, Torres, Simoes

U.S.S.R.
Yashin, Ponomarev, Korneev, Khurtsilava, Danilov, Voronin, Sichinava, Metreveli, Malofeev, Banishevskiy, Serebrjannikov

Referee: K. Dagnall (England). *Scorers:* Eusebio (pen.), Torres (Portugal)
Malofeev (U.S.S.R.)
Attendance 70,000

Final

ENGLAND 4, WEST GERMANY 2 (1-1)　　　　　　*Wembley, 30 July*
(after extra time: 2-2 after 90 minutes)
ENGLAND
Banks, Cohen, Wilson, J. Charlton, Moore, Stiles, R. Charlton, Ball, Hunt, Hurst, Peters

WEST GERMANY
Tilkowski, Höttges, Schulz, Weber, Schnellinger, Haller, Beckenbauer, Seeler, Held, Overath, Emmerich

Referee: G. Dienst (Switzerland). *Scorers:* Hurst (3), Peters (England)
Haller, Weber (W. Germany)
Attendance 93,000

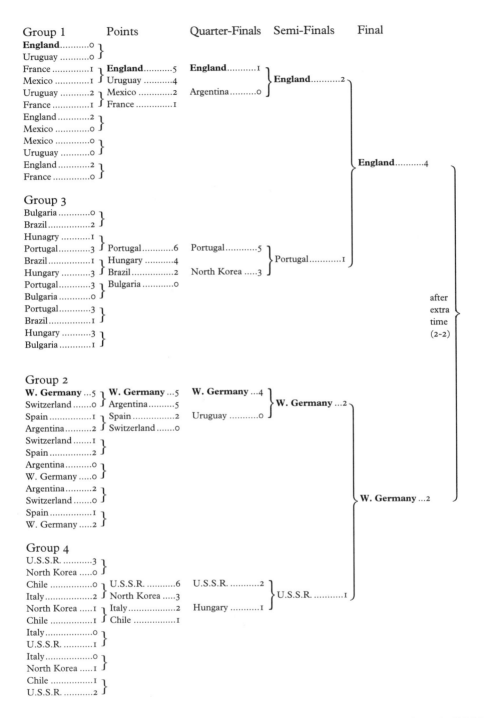

Third Place: Portugal 2 U.S.S.R. 1

Acknowledgements

The co-operation of many members of the 1966 squad, kindly providing their reminiscences, has added much to the recollection of events, and I would like to give them my grateful thanks. Thanks are due to the *Sunday Telegraph* for an extract from one of my interviews with Pelé; to Steve Dobell for being an enthusiastic editor; and, especially, to Franz Beckenbauer, a formidable player, authoritative captain, a shrewd manager, generous opponent, and valued friend to all who were fortunate to know him during a long and successful career, for providing the Foreword.

The following publications were referred to in the preparation of the text:

FA Year Book, 1950-1986 (Heinemann and Pelham); *World Cup 1962* (Saunders/Heinemann); *A Funny Thing Happened on My Way to Spurs* (Greaves/Kaye, 1962); *World Cup '66* (McIlvanney/ Eyre and Spottiswoode); *World Soccer Magazine* (Jan–Dec 1966); *Forward for England* (Charlton/Pelham, 1967); *For Leeds and England* (Charlton/Stanley Paul, 1967); *The Magic Sponge* (Shepherdson/Pelham, 1967); *England! England!* (Moore/Stanley Paul, 1970); *Sir Alf Ramsey, Anatomy of a Football Manager* (Marquis/Arthur Barker, 1970); *Mexico '70* (Peters/Cassell); *World Cup 1970* (Miller/Heinemann); *Father of Football* (Miller/Stanley Paul, 1970); *Let's Be Honest* (Greaves and Gutteridge/Pelham, 1972); *Bobby Moore* (Moore/Everest, 1976); *Football Worlds* (Rous/Faber, 1978); *'This One's on Me'* (Greaves/Arthur Barker, 1979); *Boys of '66* (Tyler/Hamlyn, 1981); *Cup Magic* (Miller/ Sidgwick and Jackson, 1981); *Rothman's Yearbook, 1985-86* (Queen Anne Press).

The photographs in this book are reproduced by permission of the following: Associated Press: pages 5(al), 6(a); Gerry Cranham: 1; TPS/Keystone: 5(ar), 8(a); TPS/Central Press: 14; Popperfoto: 7(a&b), 8(b), 15(a), 16(a); Syndication International: 2–3, 6(b), 9(a&b), 15(b); Topham: 4, 5(b), 12–13, 16(b); Press Association: 10–11.